Sense or Nonsense

Sense or Nonsense

Contemporary Education at the Crossroads

Bert Case Diltz

McClelland and Stewart Limited

© 1972 McClelland and Stewart Limited

ALL RIGHTS RESERVED

0-7710-2815-6

The Canadian Publishers
McClelland and Stewart Limited
25 Hollinger Road, Toronto 374

Printed and Bound in Canada

Contents

Foreword

This little book is addressed to people who still believe in education, to people who recognize the supremacy of mind over matter. The true aim of education is to nourish and cultivate the mind. It is the mature and disciplined mind that is the main source of responsibility for the betterment of life and the care of the living. *Sense or Nonsense* is addressed to parents and students who acknowledge that much can be learned from the study of great literature, and that life squandered in mindless emotionalism is a sinful waste of human potential.

From beginning to end this book is concerned with the study of lyric poetry, poetic drama, and the language of artistic composition. It is not a text that presumes to dictate methods of teaching, but rather a collection of ideas, insights, and suggestions that may lead students to look beneath the images and rhythms for the intuitions latent in great poetry.

In one respect, *Sense or Nonsense* is an extension and intensification of theories presented in *The Sense of Wonder*, and the poems chosen for study may be found in current anthologies such as *Word Magic, New Horizons,* and *Poetic Experience* where some of the best British, Canadian, and American poetry has been gathered together.

In order to appreciate the importance of the study of poetry, it is necessary to examine the climate prevailing in the schools. The views expressed in the introductory chapters are intended to give some idea of the weight of cumulus beneath which genuine poetry struggles towards the light. The concluding chapters suggest ways and means of scattering the clouds and dispelling the mists that pollute the air.

Why, it may be asked, should poetry be taken seriously in today's technological world? Along with the study of mathematics, it nourishes the intellectual life of thinking people and keeps the fervour for speculation and wonder alive. It is free of ulterior motives. Its sole aim is to be faithful to the poet's thrust.

The study of poetry has nothing to do with job security, teacher accountability, or orgies of emotional indulgence. It has everything to do with the quickening of the imagination and the expansion of its capacity for surmise. Genuine poetry may provide the touchstone necessary to test and expose the sham of exploiting poetic forms to glamorize materialism and cultural superficiality. The antidote to mediocrity is excellence.

Through the centuries the ideas of wise and learned men and women have been gathered together in the libraries of the world. A small but vital part of that great treasure is made available in the schools. It represents a portion of our heritage and is an essential ingredient of the cultivated mind. To direct attention to the values that may accrue from such study is the responsibility of all concerned with education.

Sense or Nonsense is also an appeal to those who are confused by the fulminations of contemporary educational theorists to stand fast by their beliefs and to refresh their spirits and reaffirm their hopes by contemplating such a vision as the following:

I Did But Prompt

I did but prompt the age to quit their clogs
    By the known rules of ancient liberty,
    When straight a barbarous noise environs me
    Of owls and cuckoos, asses, apes, and dogs;
As when those hinds that were transformed to frogs
    Railed at Latona's twin-born progeny,
    Which after held the Sun and Moon in fee.
    But this is got by casting pearls to hogs,
That bawl for freedom in their senseless mood,
    And still revolt when Truth would set them free.
    Licence they mean when they cry Liberty;
For who loves that, must first be wise and good;
    But from that mark how far they rove we see,
    For all this waste of wealth, and loss of blood.

                      – John Milton (1608-74)

With no idea to what their speculations are leading, the theorists are hell-bent in the name of freedom to challenge the authority of the law, reason, and common sense. Through the centuries, however, theorists have come and gone and left behind little but their own frustrations. In spite of them bright and willing students have found food for thought in the classrooms and workshops of the schools, and the dull and disgruntled have remained bewildered. The psychologists and sociologists may classify and corral the less talented and encourage them to accept their lot, but they cannot make students of those who have little aptitude for learning. Must the whole system of education be modified in order to accommodate their whims or unstructured tantrums? Without restraining banks a river loses its identity. Whether the student works with language or with lathe, he is in school to organize and develop his mental faculties. The theorist, on the other hand, would drive him along the road to chaos without a creed.

Whatever else is lost in the morass of the experimenters, the study of literature must be preserved. It is time for those who believe in real education to stand fast together. The Scots have a lovely lilting word for it: *craigélachié*.

B.C.D.

Sense or Nonsense

I

The Creative Imagination
and the Educational System

It has been said that our educational system is one of the finest products of democracy in the Twentieth Century. How can we keep it so? How can many more good teachers be secured and trained? How can the education of both the pupil and the teacher, be improved? What is the difference between instruction and education? How can more creative thought be released into the stream? What is the nature of creative thinking and what conditions are favourable to its production? Should the "bright" be grouped? How can the uniqueness of individual personality be protected against exploitation? How can educational standards be raised? These are some of the questions on which comment is now proposed.

Good morale is the best teaching aid yet devised, and morale among high school teachers in Ontario is high. Here are young men and women, full of vigour and spontaneity, conscientious and dedicated. In spite of criticism occasionally leveled against teachers, this province is blessed with a great deal of imaginative, inspired, and creative teaching.

With fair salary scales, social security and prestige, good working conditions and adequate pensions, many young people have been attracted into secondary school teaching. They have found the work satisfying, self-realizing, and challenging. In a few years they will be quite the equals of the good old-timers who have left the scene. But had these benefits not been forthcoming, conditions would be far different in the schools today.

Expansion of facilities and services is not the only challenge confronting the educational system today. Much more profound in significance and far-reaching in effect are the ideas emerging from the shift of emphasis from the group to the individual, from the dictating of attitudes to the cultivating of aptitudes, from many electives to a few carefully selected subjects of concentration, from the imitation of thought to the initiation of thinking, from the perfecting of skills to the disclosing of the principles on which the practices are founded. The sociological approach to education has led to a quagmire of adjustment to standardized mediocrity and of conformity to a homogenized society from which education is now struggling to extricate itself. We talk a great deal about individual differences, and in practice we appear to ignore them or to obliterate them altogether. At heart the school has always been sound, but it has been asked to bear so many extraneous social burdens that it has had little energy left to perform its real duties. The teacher is not a social worker but a scholar whose greatest service to society at all levels of education is expressed through the exactness of his scholarship and the expertness of his skill in stirring other minds to think. The pupil is not a young citizen whose mind is to be moulded to the shape of a preconceived ideology. Men and women, boys and girls, teachers and pupils are confronted today by demands upon their intelligence such as the world has not seen before. And education, let it be remembered, is not a mass effort, but an individual matter. It has to do with persons, not with tough-mindedness nor with tender-mindedness, or any other mannerism, but with *real* persons, people who use their brains to steer a practical course through the traffic jams of daily problems.

In 1687 Isaac Newton published his *Principia Mathematica* which stated among other things:

"Absolute, true, and mathematical time, of itself and from its own nature, flows equably without relation to anything external."

"Absolute space, in its own nature, without relation to anything external, remains always similar and immovable."

These ideas were serviceable in their time, but in good classical tradition they divided nature into several parts. Einstein challenged these concepts and eventually, after a series of surprisingly simple experiments based on not so simple patterns of thought and imagination, put forth the idea that space and time are interrelated and are part of the same reality. To tamper with one is to affect the other. This led in 1905 to his famous formula $E = mc^2$, where E is energy content, m is mass (which varies according to speed) and c is the velocity of light. Since then the world of man has not been the same. Einstein's experiments confirmed the essential unity of all nature, changed our conception of the physical universe, and extended the horizons of the human mind. The theories of Newton and Einstein are related to each other. The past, the present, and the future belong to a single individual whole.

In the years that Einstein's idea has been at work we have witnessed a series of explosions in human thought. This chain reaction may go on for centuries to come. It could revolutionize the whole educational system, since it confirms the unity of all knowledge and of all peoples and reaffirms the potentiality and sanctity of the individual mind. In more ways than one education may be moving from a classical era to a glassical era, since many windows are needed to throw light on Einstein's fourth dimension, his new space-time dimension. Not only are we witnessing upheavals in mathematical thinking today, but in thinking about language as well some extremely salutary streams are washing away a lot of rubble, especially from the field

of education. Einstein once proclaimed "Perfection of tools
and confusion of aims are characteristic of our time." And
since aims are not aims until they are stated in language,
it may here be added that confusion in language means
a confusion in thinking. Such phrases as "directional goals,"
"objective consequences," "testable hypotheses," and
"theoretical orientations" set up short circuits in the mind
and not infrequently blow emotional fuses. When thought
is complex, they may be hard to avoid, but one aim of
education is to encourage people to think in terms of concrete objects and events rather than in the terms of woolly
generalizations. Imagine the result, had Lincoln at Gettys-
burg begun "Eight and seven-tenths decades ago the
pioneer workers in this continental area implemented a
new group based on an ideology of free boundaries and
initial equality" and ended "That political supervision of
the integrated units, for the integrated units, by the integrated units, shall not become null and void on the superficial area of this planet." Einstein's thesis invites us all
to look again at things, to observe exactly, to name precisely, and to listen less to the windbaggery of those who
would deceive.

"The first sensation an infant gets" wrote William James,
"is for him the universe. ... the infant encounters an
object in which all the categories of the intellect are combined." George Johnston, the poet-professor at Carleton
University expresses this idea beautifully in the leading
poem of his collection *The Cruising Auk* (Oxford), but he
probes farther and more deeply into the mystery to give
us a fresh insight into our human predicament.

The Pool

A boy gazing in a pool
Is all profound; his eyes are cool
And he's as though unborn, he's gone;
He's the abyss he gazes on.

A man searches the pool in vain
For his profundity again;
He finds it neither there nor here
And all between is pride and fear.

His eyes are warm with love and death,
Time makes a measure of his breath;
The world is now profound and he
Fearful, on its periphery.

– George Johnston
from *The Cruising Auk*
Oxford University Press 1959

A pathetic and hopeless predicament, you may think: a recommendation that the infantile strain in our nature be prolonged. But here is a new insight latent with truth and charged with power to create fruitful thinking. That, too, is an aim of education; indeed, it is the chief aim of the whole blessed system from the kindergarten to the graduate school, from the cradle to the grave, to nourish our thinking, and feeling, and imagining on thought-evoking insights. "Science and poetry have the same root in human nature," claimed A. N. Whitehead. Mathematics and literature are more than a body of knowledge, a collection of unprofitable problems and improbable rhythms; they are methods of very serious inquiry into the nature of man and his environment. As pupils move from one grade to another in the study of mathematics and literature, they increase the number and deepen the quality of their insights into the nature of the mathematical and the literary methods of inquiry. In education the process is often as important as the product. We all participate whole-heartedly in life without having much knowledge of its meaning. We strive to appease our innate appetite for perfection without the power to conceive the form. Works of genius, whether in mathematical or aesthetic form, are consolations to all who can enter into them. It is education that unlocks the door.

Both the creative thinker in mathematics and the creative thinker in one of the arts extract ideas from the natural phenomena they observe, and then express their insights in symbols, the language of numbers or the language of words, lines, colours, or sounds. Each one, even' the "abstract" artist, adds importantly to the unity of all knowledge. The teacher as artist in the classroom is both an instructor and an educator. As instructor (*instruere* = to pile up or build) he provides information and direction. He organizes material just as an engineer builds a bridge or a lawyer constructs a case. As an educator (*educare* = to nourish) he cultivates the mind even as a gardener cultivates the soil in which a plant is growing. Between instruction and education there is no opposition, except that education goes farther and deeper. It leads to more significant ends because the pupil, like the plant, must organize and assimilate the material on which he feeds. The teacher cannot organize it for him. Like a sensitive plant, the pupil is a highly selective feeder. He takes what he wants or needs and leaves a great deal untouched that has no meaning for him at the moment. No two feed in the same way or need exactly the same kind or combination of nourishment. Each one digests what to him is palatable, i.e. what he can organize into useful knowledge and what he can fit into his pattern of experience. In some respects the pupil's independence of spirit sits in judgment on his understanding. This is his personal right, and it should be respected. He may be deceived by false subject-matter, but he should never be master-minded by his teacher. Let it never be forgotten that a good reason for the pupil's presence in school is to develop his mental faculties.

"Nothing in education is so astonishing as the amount of ignorance it accumulates in the form of inert facts." This quotation from *The Education of Henry Adams* is a warn-

ing to all teachers not to lose sight of the real end of education. How often in arithmetic and grammar and scientific
experiment, the principle behind the practice is overlooked
or forgotten in the flurry of storing the memory with what
Whitehead called "the pretentious names for obvious
facts," and then added "knowledge dispersed does not go
deep enough to be interesting!" Knowledge that is not
rooted in the verification, rather than the variation, of
observation, is as useless as tumbleweed. Facts are alive
when they direct thought; inert facts smother it. It is the
end result that makes learning significant; the depth of
understanding to which the insight leads, rather than the
breadth of information with which the reason becomes
encumbered.

If the school is envisaged as a hive of thinkers, gathering
the honey of insights and bringing experience to book,
it may be appropriate to try to find out what thinking
is, and what conditions are favourable to creative thought.
Reasoning is the organization of ideas according to the
laws of association and with a specific end in view. When
images and ideas flow together and combine to form new
and often surprising patterns the thinker's imagination
is at work. The creative imagination is operative when the
parts of one pattern are transposed effectively to another
pattern. The imagination has suddenly created a new pattern. To this mental activity a variety of names has been
given such as inspiration, flashes of vision, sudden insight,
leaps of sympathy, moments of confidence or foreboding.
Such moments will not come when they are called, but
when they do come, we must be quick to catch them in
flight. Sir Maurice Bowra writing in *The Prophetic Element*
says "Vision is often more vivid and more obviously trust-
worthy than what comes through the senses." This mental
activity has nothing to do with "I.Q." tests or rote learning.
The creative imagination is a complement to the reason.
Creative thinking has been defined as "a type of thinking

illustrated in the production of a work of art or the solution of a scientific problem." Let us now observe in imagination a creative artist at work.

Earle Birney, a poet-professor at various Universities, published in *The Atlantic Monthly* for June 1959 an eight-line poem that he entitled *Ellesmereland*. Begging the poet's pardon, I should like to suggest one way by which this literary gem may have come into existence. I claim the protection of the court by stating that this fiction has no foundation in fact. Hardly has man won freedom from his subservience to nature, it is supposed, than he becomes a victim of the will of his fellow man. There are people and nations that would make man a captive creature, brain-wash his mind in their doctrines and make him over to suit their needs. The next step would be the making of a whole man, a living robot. Speculating on this idea, a poet turns back to nature to see how nature's creatures thrive. In the process of this preparation to think, this incubating of an idea, this illuminating of a pattern, and this verification of an idea in the form of a finished poem, the poet may well have "seen red" and then cooled off to see a startling contrast in black and white. Once his mind set to work, he shaped a spearhead with a razor's edge. This is what he wrote:

Ellesmereland

Explorers say that harebells rise
from the cracks of Ellesmereland
and cod swim fat beneath the ice
that grinds its groaning strand
No man is settled on that coast
The harebells are alone
Nor is there talk of making man
from ice cod bell or stone

−Earle Birney
The Atlantic Monthly
June 1959, p. 64

This insight is presented in terse words and tangible images, and these words and images pinpoint the attention and concentrate the mind on the poet's central meaning. The poet worked toward this unity; the reader works from it. Too often, however, the reader may be misled into wondering why the poet omitted all commas and periods and fail completely to discover the poet's comment on the audacity and futility of man in the face of Nature's primitive forces.

Just as the production of this little masterpiece probably did a great deal for the poet in helping him clear out a lot of intellectual and emotional rubbish from his mind, the study of it can likewise clean up a lot of loose thinking and feeling in the reader's mind. Aristotle called this process catharsis. This is one reason that the visions of men of genius are more important than the views of economists and social scientists. When such insights are free to be apprehended, why confine the mind to a discussion of rhythms and rhymes? We learn by flashes of insight. A dog or a horse may be *trained* by habit-forming drills; a boy becomes *educated* by flashes of insight into the meaning of things. What conditions are favourable to creative thinking?

1. Time to think; freedom from the excitement of constant activity; release from repetitive, nose-to-the-grindstone, homework exercises that exhaust without enlightening. Time to browse, to reflect, to refocus points of view, to let the mind stretch itself and grow.
2. The cultivation of wide-awake attention when new discoveries are in the making.
3. An urge to try new ways of solving old problems.
4. The assignment of a problem worth solving or a task challenging enough and personally rewarding enough to warrant an expenditure of mental energy.
5. The realization of the great personal satisfaction to be

derived from doing a good job. This is the urge that drives the scientist to his goal and the artist to the completion of his work, in spite of all kinds of hardship and personal sacrifice.

6. Time to relax concentration and to indulge in activities far removed from the basic work itself.

7. The careful imitative study of good models of mathematical and linguistic patterns of thought.

Now, it may be asked, are all pupils and students gifted? And is it the business of the school to make scientists and artists? Certainly not! But in every normal youngster there is a bit of flint which, when struck by the right ideas, will give forth a spark. Or as Whitehead has said, "Some measure of genius is the rightful inheritance of every man." Perhaps in the secondary school at least, more time should be devoted to education and less to instruction. Perhaps teachers should teach less and teach it in a more inspiring way. This procedure might alter considerably the normal grading within a class.

Should "bright" pupils be segregated and taught separately? It has already been disclosed that ability grouping does not give academic advantage. But who are the bright ones? Are they the right ones? How were they discovered? What is to be done with them? Who is to do it? What would have been done with or to a young Shelley, Byron, Blake, or Burns, had any one of these appeared in a class last year? Who would presume to organize genius out of existence? In a democracy, moreover, segregation is a denial of a basic human right. An intellectual elite is helpless unless it commands the respect of the masses.

In the curriculum there is already enough to challenge, even inspire, the brightest pupil, and if he is really gifted he can get along faster without a teacher at all. Both these points have been illustrated again and again. But let it not be forgotten that genius is known by its fruits and not by its flowers. Records show that the majority of gifted people in the arts and sciences reached the peak of quality in their productions between 30 and 40 years of age; in architecture and exploration, between 40 and 50; in military strategy, between 50 and 60; and in political sagacity, statesmanship, and administration, between 60 and 70. In all these different activities, the gifted one expressed himself long after the sun had set on his formal schooling. A double standard in education would soon lead to no standard at all.

If anyone wishes seriously to help all pupils, he can do so best by helping the teacher to improve his teaching in the classroom where mind meets mind. One area for this activity could be the curriculum, and the other, teacher education, and whether we like it or not, both areas should be of national concern. When a teacher from each of the following grades, grade 3, 6, 9, 12, 15, and 18 meets together with his opposite numbers to discuss and organize courses of study in Mathematics, or Science, or the English language, something revolutionary is likely to happen to the course of study and to the aims of education. When teachers from the various levels come together to discuss teacher education, some hope may dawn that we can meet our educational obligation to the nation confidently. The individuals in these groups will be doing something rare. They will be thinking about education in a vertical pattern rather than a horizontal plane. And they will be furthering the cause of national unity. Teacher recruitment and teacher education in a rapidly expanding system are of sufficient national importance to warrant the extension of federal grants.

Reference has twice been made to poet-professors and it may be thought by some that every teacher should himself be a creative artist. This might not be a bad idea, but we have not enough Ned Pratt's to go around. Many teachers at all levels may lack the ability to engage productively in artistic or scientific achievement, but all good teachers in their own personal way can serve valiantly the cause of the humanities which must be renewed in every generation.

For every generation of pupils and students the great minds of the past are brought to life again by its teachers. The character of the nation is shaped and coloured by the creative imagination of its people, and every individual thread in the warp and woof of the fabric has its important part to play. How strange that there has been only one Shakespeare and one Churchill! History has shown again and again that everyone of us is in some degree indispensable. Robert Frost has expressed this belief in memorable form:

The Road Not Taken

Two roads diverged in a yellow wood,
And sorry I could not travel both
And be one traveller, long I stood
And I looked down one as far as I could
To where it bent in the undergrowth;

—

Then took the other, as just as fair,
And having perhaps the better claim,
Because it was grassy and wanted wear;
Though as for that the passing there
Had worn them really about the same.

—

And both that morning equally lay
In leaves no step had trodden black.
Oh, I kept the first for another day!
Yet knowing how way leads on to way,
I doubted if I should ever come back.

—

I shall be telling this with a sigh
Somewhere ages and ages hence:
Two roads diverged in a wood, and I–
I took the one less travelled by,
And that has made all the difference.

– Robert Frost

Life is composed of many such moments of decision, and they accumulate and grow into what we call character and describe as maturity. Here in four stanzas of plain and rhythmic language is another of those profound insights into life for which the heart hungers. And it is proof enough that something from each one of us survives the crisis of the grave.

II

Creature Creative

The history of education is the story of continually changing aims and purposes. At the present time a veritable
revolution in both the matter and the method of education
is in the making. The source of its power is the rediscovery
of the unity of all nature, the unity of all knowledge, and
the unity of individual personality. Astute observers are
proclaiming that "the creative arts may be the new forms
which could be the living contemporary expression of the
eternal truths."* The creative arts may provide a way by
which mankind can find harmony and unity. The art of
teaching may also be creative. It can help to shape a reader's
intellectual, emotional, and imaginative response and keep
his experience viable. How can a work of literary art be
recognized?

By comparing two passages in which two writers
attempt to deal with the same subject, it will be possible
to distinguish quickly between what is a work of art and
what is not. The two passages should first be read against
each other without comment:

I.   *The Scarecrow*

A scarecrow stood in a field one day
     Stuffed with straw,
     Stuffed with hay,

---

*Editorial in *Education for Teaching* (November 1959) Journal of the Association
of Teachers in Colleges and Departments of Education.

He watched the folk on the king's highway,
　　But never a word said he.

Much he saw but naught did heed,
　　Knowing not night,
　　Knowing not day,
For, having naught, did nothing need,
　　And never a word said he.

A little grey mouse had made its nest,
　　Oh so wee,
　　Oh so grey,
In a sleeve of a coat that was poor Tom's best
　　But the scarecrow naught said he.

His hat was the home of a small jenny wren,
　　Ever so sweet,
　　Ever so gay,
A squirrel had put by his fear of men,
　　And hissed him, but naught needed he.

Ragged old man, I loved him well,
　　Stuffed with straw,
　　Stuffed with hay;
Many's the tale he could tell,
　　But never a word says he.

　　　　　　　　– Michael Franklin

II.　　　*The Scarecrow*

All winter through I bow my head
　　Beneath the driving rain;
The North Wind powders me with snow
　　And blows me black again;
At midnight in a maze of stars
　　I flame with glittering rime,
And stand, above the stubble, stiff
　　As mail at morning-prime.

But when that child, called Spring, and all
     His host of children, come,
Scattering their buds and dew upon
     These acres of my home,
Some rapture in my rags awakes;
     I lift void eyes and scan
The skies for crows, those ravening foes,
     Of my strange master, Man.
I watch him striding lank behind
     His clashing team, and know
Soon will the wheat swish body high
     Where once lay sterile snow;
Soon shall I gaze across a sea
     Of sun-begotten grain,
Which my unflinching watch hath sealed
     For harvest once again

— Walter de la Mare

In reading *Scarecrow I* the attention is divided and scattered among a mouse, an old coat, a wren, and a squirrel. We get a view of things associated with one scarecrow that the writer thinks he has observed. In *Scarecrow II* attention is focused, and nothing is allowed to detract from the central image. The poet has caught a vision of a scarecrow and writes of something felt rather than observed. In *I*, form is imposed on the sense; in *II*, form follows the sense. In *I* rhymes are often inept and rhythms clumsy and stilted. In *II* rhymes are natural to the sense, and the poem follows a steadily rising rhythm. The last line of each stanza in *I* is pointless, and some other lines are trite. We blush for the writer of *Oh so wee, Oh so grey, Ever so sweet, Ever so gay.* Here is abundant evidence of poor craftsmanship — a mere list of supposedly child-delighting ideas strung together without skill, feeling, or felicity of language. The whole composition is based on a false assumption that children are entertained by such fabrication. They are, as every teacher knows, quick to detect the insincerity of posturing.

In *Scarecrow II* an artist stands poised in the midst of his subject. He writes under a compulsion to write and the result is the organic unity of a work of art. Nothing can be added or taken away. The language is alive and felicitous: *powders me with snow, glittering rime, rapture in my rags, void eyes, clashing team,* and *swish body high* are all imaginative phrases that remain to haunt the mind and to keep the scarecrow alive in the mind long after the poem has been read. Such composition, like prayer, is the most composing of activities. The most astonishing difference between the two passages, however, is the discovery that *I* is set forth in a horizontal plane of feeble thought, and that *II* is built in a vertical pattern of thinking, feeling, and imagining.

A careful reading of the two following poems may clarify further the difference between poetry and verse.

I   *Mine-sweeping Trawlers*

Not ours the fighter's glory,
    The glory and the praise;
Unnoticed to and fro
    We pass our dangerous ways.

We sift the drifting sea
    And blindly grope beneath;
Obscure and toilsome we,
    The fishermen of death.

But when the great ships go
    To battle through the gloom,
Our hearts beat high to know
    We cleared their path of doom.
                    − E. Hilton Young

II   *Mine Sweepers*

Dawn off the Foreland − the young flood making
    Jumbled and short and steep −
Black in the hollows and bright where it's breaking −

Awkward water to sweep.
"Mines reported in the fairway,
"Warn all traffic and detain.
"'Sent up *Unity, Claribel, Assyrian, Stormcock,* and *Golden Gain.*"

Noon off the Foreland — The first ebb making
Lumpy and strong in the bight.
Boom after boom, and the golf-hut shaking
And the jackdaws wild with fright!
"Mines located in the fairway,
"Boats now working up the chain,
"Sweepers — *Unity, Claribel, Assyrian, Stormcock,* and *Golden Gain.*"

Dusk off the Foreland — the last light going
And the traffic crowding through,
And five damned trawlers with their syrens blowing
Heading the whole review!
"Sweep completed in the fairway.
"No more mines remain.
"'Sent back *Unity, Claribel, Assyrian, Stormcock,* and *Golden Gain.*"

— Rudyard Kipling

For convenience the first passage will be referred to as *Trawlers* and the second as *Sweepers.* Although *Trawlers* is written in the first person, it reveals no evidence of personal involvement. What should be regarded as a serious subject is presented in the jingle of light verse. The language is trite and hackneyed, *great ships, hearts beat high, path of doom,* and the inversion in *toilsome we* is artificial. In every respect *Trawlers* is shallow and lacking in imaginative depth. Nothing is particularized. The writer claims that the work is dangerous, but he fails to make the reader feel danger. Without conviction of feeling or evidence of creative compulsion the account is sterile, colourless, and worthless. It is the kind of vague, unrealistic "sing-song" verse to be found in children's picture books where it corrupts their natural taste for poetry.

Sweepers, on the other hand, is a direct telegrammic report that leaves the reader free to feel the experience. The matter-of-fact terseness sharpens the tension, the reality, and the urgency. *Dawn, Noon,* and *Dusk* preserve the unity. Felicity of language,*jumbled, awkward, lumpy,* presents choppy seas that can be seen and felt. A grim and exciting undertone compresses the factual and dramatic account into a vertical pattern. Action is narrated, but comment is withheld. In contrast *Trawlers* is an impersonal and phony reflection of sentimentality lolling in a horizontal plane.

A masterpiece of literary art is built or grows in a vertical pattern rather than on a horizontal plane. If we examine this presupposition, we may presently see what a variety of important implications it directs at all our practices in reading and writing creatively.

The word vertical finds its root in *vortex,* meaning whirlpool. In the context of a work of art such as Shakespeare's *Macbeth* or *Hamlet,* Hardy's *The Mayor of Casterbridge,* or Constance Holme's *The Lonely Plough,* Rebecca West's short story, *The Salt of the Earth,* or Katherine Mansfield's *The Doll's House,* Robert Lynd's essay *The Kitten,* Coleridge's famous poem *The Rhyme of the Ancient Mariner,* or any popularly admired sonnet or lyric by a creative artist old or new; in the context of any one of these, a vertical pattern means that at the time of composition, thought, feeling, and imagining were all churned up in the author's mind to an apex, crown, or zenith. At the centre was then, and remains now, a core of experience, a living self-creating cell, an enzyme, like a tornado's ominous heart, moving with a whirlpool's turbulence. It is a whole made up of parts that lie one on top of another like vertebrae conjoined and held erect by a spinal theme. Every segment is essential to the functioning of the whole, and each disc, or word, or image is in a way an epitome of the whole, but interrelated with its neighbours. The whole is an integrated pattern, an artistic unit, a new experience, like Dylan

Thomas's *Fern Hill*, metaphorically pollinated and many dimensional. Out of the fission and fusion in the author's catalytic brain came an essence, a climax of feeling, a new thing unseen before but born of the author's sacrifice of himself to the masterpiece produced. It has depth and height, and a life of its own. Its meaning and its being are one and the same. It can embrace and accommodate the intangibles, and like a fountain, spray the atmosphere of the mind with imaginative suggestion or drench it with disturbing abstraction. Its saturation is complete. A literary masterpiece can regenerate itself and radiate and extend its own meaning through metaphor and parable to succeeding generations of readers. It can lift the mind's eye from things seen and said to things unseen but meant. It can disclose the yearnings of the spirit and create a twilight world of wonder.

The word horizontal, by contrast and complement, finds its root in *horizon*, meaning limit or boundary. In the context in which the word is presently used it has more to do with space and time than with essences. In a literary work that trails off in a horizonal plane, thought, feeling, and imagining are spread out end to end within conceivable limits or boundaries, like chequered linoleum, with little connection except that of repetition between the designs. In a horizontal plane what might have become a work of art disintegrates, and thought degenerates into a way of feeling. A series of events may drift leisurely across the mind, like clouds across the sky; but there is no pillar of fire to lead the reader on. The reader may encounter a mood, but not apprehend an experience. At best he may be confronted by a record of an experience that was never fully felt by the writer. It is unchallenging because unchanneled. As a work of art it is sterile. It is concerned with peripheries, not a core. It admits of the expansion and contraction of one component or element at the expense of another. Parts may function separately outside its boundaries; and the mind of the reader may wander away into by-paths of fugitive speculation, sometimes interesting in themselves, become lost, and never find its way back to any highroad of thought. Some works of historical fiction fall into this category.

But not all works in a horizontal plane are fragmentary. Some have unity, but are not dynamic. *The Riddle of the Sands* and *Rogue Male* are well written and make interesting reading, but they are not works of art. From them the reader would never learn "to behold life with the synoptic vision of a visionary art at its highest." These stories are mere chains of events with a little character-drawing thrown in. Neither one rises to a climax; it just ends because it has apparently gone far enough. And, furthermore, detective fiction raises problems that are always and completely solved within the terms in which the problems are set. Such stories are horizontal, exhaustive, and conclusive. A work of great literary art, on the other hand, is open at both ends. *The Mayor of Casterbridge,* for example, solves nothing, but suggests a great deal. It raises questions, but it is content to leave them unanswered. It reveals the predicament of man in his creatureship and in the complexity of life's problems.

The following brief paragraph from the book will, I hope, illustrate what is meant by a vertical pattern in a work of art – at least one important phase of it. The story deals with the rise and fall of Michael Henchard. It begins with his coming up a country road out of the wilderness of nonentity; it ends with his going down a country road into the wilderness of oblivion. The whole story in all its phases is concerned with that coming and going. Here is an incidental paragraph taken from a minor episode in the story which imitates and keeps alive in the reader's mind that fateful transition. Hardy could have omitted it without affecting the facts of his story; but it was essential to the deepening of his theme.

When Elizabeth-Jane opened the hinged casement next morning, the mellow air brought in the feel of imminent autumn almost as distinctly as if she had been in the remotest hamlet. Casterbridge was the complement of the rural life around: not its urban opposite. Bees and butterflies in the corn-fields at the top of the town, who desired to get to the meads at the bottom, took no circuitous course, and flew straight down High Street without any apparent consciousness that they were traversing strange latitudes. And in autumn airy spheres of thistledown floated into the same street, lodged upon the shop fronts, blew into drains; and innumerable tawny and yellow leaves skimmed along the pavement, and stole through people's doorways into their passages, with a hesitating scratch on the floor, like the skirts of timid visitors.

– Thomas Hardy, *The Mayor of Casterbridge*, Ch. ix

For similar reasons, among others, Shakespeare's major dramas and de la Mare's lyrics, for example, are works of art. As we read, we do not feel that we are being managed into a position, socially improved, or made against our wills the recipients of anybody's propaganda or dialectic. We are not so much informed as transformed by our reading of imaginative literature. Our feelings are not defined for us but refined by the literary or imaginative experience through which we pass. And that is the real meaning of experience. It is a process of passing through a mental activity. It is not only what happens to us but what we do with what happens to us. It is a testing by personal contact of the validity of a joy or sorrow projected by the artist into our minds. We move in much the same direction that the author took, and we take steps very nearly like his own.

"Experience is never limited, and it is never complete; it is an immense sensibility, a kind of huge spider-web of the finest silken threads suspended in the chamber of consciousness, and catching every air-borne particle in its tissue."

– Henry James, *Partial Portraits*

Appreciation involves one in appraisal and evaluation, and often from Grades 6 to 13 it means judging a work of art that has not been experienced, perhaps not even read carefully, or perchance seen only through the eyes of a teacher or the opinion of a critic. Compare an appraisal of Milton's use of the sonnet form in *On His Blindness* with the experiencing, even vicariously, of Milton's thoughts and feelings in his distress, and you will see the difference between the two words and a reason why "experience" should take precedence over "appreciation" as an objective in the study of literature.

In *Macbeth* the witches proclaim

> Fair is foul, and foul is fair

And presently we hear Macbeth himself using the same words

> So foul and fair a day I have not seen.

And we are already launched into a sea where good and evil may become indistinguishable.

Lady Macbeth, reading the letter in Act I, and Lady Macbeth, sleepwalking in Act V, are one and the same person, and the two dramatic situations are securely and subtly connected in the vertical pattern.

Again in Act I Macbeth's first words to his wife are:

Macbeth:	My dearest love, Duncan comes here tonight.
Lady Macbeth:	And when goes hence?
Macbeth:	Tomorrow, as he purposes.
Lady Macbeth:	O! never Shall sun that morrow see.

In Act V Macbeth's first words on learning of his wife's death are:

> She should have died hereafter;
> There would have been a *time* for such a word.
> *Tomorrow,* and *tomorrow,* and *tomorrow,*
> Creeps in this petty pace from day to day,
> To the last syllable of recorded *time;*

Macbeth's references to time are significant and not accidental. When he replies to Lady Macbeth, he is still a free man, free to choose between the killing of his king and the protecting of the life of his kingly guest. But now "tomorrow" and the freedom to decide what may be done tomorrow have been taken from him. Nothing is left but time, and time is running out in a meaningless extension of itself. Here again are both vertical pattern and metaphorical pollination.

Macbeth could not wait for time; now time cannot wait for him. His very natural human zeal for expediency is reflected in each of the three mean-minded, expedient, and obsequious opportunists that the Porter admits to his imaginary hell. Expediency, without the delay or embarrassment that might come from a choice between what is foul and what is fair, is apparently the primrose way of all professions.

The experiencing of these mental states, shaped by art into a vertical pattern, is a part of the consequence of radiation or fall-out from a great work of art. The appreciation of the characterization, plot structure, imagery, metaphor, poetic rhythms, etc., etc., is only a series of means to this end of experience, and not an end in itself.

If a work of art in words, built in a vertical pattern, may be compared to a whirlpool, writing (and thinking) in a horizontal plane, such as is found in all kinds of reports, legal documents, news stories and articles, timetables and inventories, may be compared to a pond of stagnant water, the surface of which reflects only what passes over it. Much of this horizontal writing and thinking is necessary, useful, and competent – good enough for the *practical* and *acceptable* end for which it is designed.

Horizontal thinking is sufficient for the making of money, the perpetuation of military operations, the building of pipelines, the administration of funds, the management of people and things, and the making of school timetables, but it has little to do with creative living and creative teaching. Which is better for the slow learner – a partial understanding of a page of imaginative writing or the comprehension of a page from a remedial-reading text that is correct, dull, and not worth reading anyway?

Today, we are confronted, surrounded, overwhelmed, swallowed whole by the monster called propaganda or advertising. Many of these advertisements reflect great skill in composition; they may be picturesque in language, even imaginative, but they are not works of creative art. They often exhibit a craftsmanship as great as that of the artist's; but with this difference. The two crafts, that of the propagandist or advertiser and that of the artist, differ chiefly in the purpose or end to which they are directed. Art has significance for those qualities of our minds which are concerned with the ultimate mysteries of life, among which motorcars, cigarettes, soft drinks, and other detergents can hardly be numbered. Art implies a spiritual and aesthetic effect upon the reader. It is concerned primarily with experience, and with appreciation only as a better means of apprehending experience and perceiving its excellence. Art cannot dispense with craftsmanship, but craftsmanship cannot become art until the writer (painter or composer) has some experience worth communicating. Art is built in a vertical pattern; propaganda in a horizontal plane. Art creates new mental and emotional experience; propaganda, no matter how competent, is aimed at making something known.

In the light of these opinions, let us look at our practice of writing creatively. The word creative finds its root in *creare,* meaning to make, to bring into being, to produce from nothing, to make a new thing where one did not before exist. Every human being has somewhere in his make-up a bit of flint which rightly struck will produce a spark. If God created man in His *image* this spark of inspiration, intuition, or imagination may be the divinity in man's nature — the only reality in a world of appearances. Instinctively we are all creative. We may lack the technical skill to be poets, painters, or composers, but we are at our best and happiest when engaged in creative enterprise or in the pursuit of dynamic creativeness.

Wisdom comes by flashes of insight, not by applying rules or acquiring credits. Even the child in school engages in the subtle process of selective learning. Perhaps it is his self-defence. His mind selects what it wants. And let it not be forgotten that the most important thing that happens in the classroom happens inside the pupil's head — a new insight or enlightenment, or emotional tension or satisfaction. The more he knows the more he wants to know. Interest feeds on knowledge (not the reverse) until they become identical. Mind is the most important part of personality, and the creative activity of the mind operates in a vertical pattern with little concern for spatial dimensions or time sequence. Confronted by a work of creative art, even a child finds the challenge of something greater than himself. He can participate in excellence that he may not completely understand or that his teacher cannot adequately explain. We all participate in living but no one yet has been able to explain life. The creative imagination enlarges and stretches the mind and carries it forward into new experiences. The teacher's proper function is not to oversimplify experience or to reduce truth to the understanding of the feeblest intellect. Failure to recognize this basic principle is the source of one of the most mischievous errors in modern education. It denies the existence of the creative instinct.

For nearly a century far too much emphasis has been given to the learning and practice of rules of grammar and rhetoric and not enough to the free and personal exercise of sincerity and spontaneity of statement. Language is sterile unless experienced, that is, freshly and personally felt.

The first grammar was based on the prose of Xenophon, and not on the codifications of nineteenth century rhetoricians; and the last grammar will be based on the usages of the latest creative artist in the language. Reading and writing are two sides of the same thing, and both sides in the early stages of the pupil's development should not be limited to the strictures of completeness or correctness. Our adult zeal for thoroughness, often born of fear, has carried us beyond the reaches of what is reasonable. Sentence form, for instance, should arise from thought, not thought from form. Otherwise we return to *Euphues* and to imitation rather than to intention and intuition.

There is nothing creative in the performance, even expertly, of a series of unrelated textbook exercises in grammar and rhetoric. Such practice affords little real experience in the use of the native tongue. It is only remotely connected with the actuality of everyday living. There is, on the other hand, great value in trying to set down a personal thought or feeling as briefly and tersely as possible. There is value in observing, at the direction of a teacher, the grammar and structure of one's own sentences, and in formulating rules of usage for their improvement. In doing so a child learns a good deal about language and grammar and structure in a living situation. Let it not be forgotten that language was made by man for his own use, and he can change it as his needs and tastes dictate. He is not its slave, but its master. Language is not a strait-jacket in which to confine the mind of man, but an instrument for its deliverance.

Grammar, syntax, rhetoric, word-study and sentence-form all have their place in the process of developing skill in expression, but their place is secondary. Thought is primary. In modern English, thought relationship takes precedence over linguistic relationship. No one ever learned to write by applying rules. He learned to write by having something to say. Quibbling about linguistic forms does not provide the creative activity that a young, fresh, and growing mind requires for its development. Let first things be first! First, speak, and as you speak check the logic and relationship of the words you are using. That is what adults have learned to do; children have yet to learn this skill. First, write and then see how the statement can be improved in taste and usage. What grammarian ever became a creative writer? The great writers, however, have set for us the standards of usage.

Textbooks in creative writing exhibit the same old authoritarian attitudes and dictatorial methods that have been present in teachers' minds for centuries − ever since the Greeks stopped writing intuitively and the Romans began to write by rule. These "creative" books are usually compiled by people who are not interested in writing creatively but rather in writing correctly according to their precepts of what is correct. Usage, however, changes rapidly and ruthlessly. Thought and feeling refuse to be confined to rigid and impersonal forms as cold and inhuman as a coffin. The word *creative*, if properly used, should suggest the releasing of experience.

You have all seen legal documents that are grammatically and structurally correct but that are immediately unintelligible. The teaching of composition, and that means creative writing, is the teaching of how to think, how to express thought clearly and tastefully. The teacher's job is to help pupils first of all to analyze their thought and experiences, to find out what they have discovered or observed that is worth reporting, and then to record it. We learn to play baseball by playing the game, not by reading the book of rules. We refer to the book only to clarify the finer points of the game. Likewise grammar should be applied descriptively, not prescriptively. People should be encouraged to seek a vertical rather than a horizontal approach to experience.

It may be claimed that the teacher is not teaching potential literary artists. All he wishes his pupils to achieve is an acceptable level of competence in the use of words. Such a goal is hardly worth seeking. The press, the pulpit, the platform and the radio, all exhibit a competence in quick flippancy and bland or vapid platitudes that slide ineffectually off the minds of both writer and reader or auditor. Everything is seen today through conventional eyes without the strain or discomfort of new ways of seeing. Experience passes unfocused and imagining is nonparticularized. Such abstractness dooms writing to mediocrity. Not quite one-fifth of all the writing being done today is worth reading. It might be better to leave our pupils in a blessed state of blithering illiteracy!

What exact or precise meaning does one comprehend when confronted by phrases like the following: "the open mind," "the average Canadian," "the psychological moment," "the grace of God," or "the managerial revolution"? If emphasis in composition were shifted from the observance of forms to the initiating of thought, pupils might begin to write critically and creatively. How often have we all been startled by a child's question or comment! Right there is the beginning of original thinking and creative writing. How and why that kind of thinking became suppressed in the schools is an interesting subject for speculation. Basic to any solution of the problem is a reduction in the pupil-teacher ratio.

Competence in writing can best be acquired through trying always to write creatively, i.e. by trying to make something new and fresh and personal, even in the writing of a report or a business letter. Without the presence of a mind and the imprint of a personality in the writing, composition is more likely to be dull than bright. Personal writing should be our constant aim recklessly pursued. Never was such an aim more necessary than it is today. Ponder the statement of William Blake expressed in his *Jerusalem:*

I must create a system or be enslav'd by another Man's.

III

Language Patterns

Observing the slovenly articulation of some of our glamourized heroes, their limited vocabulary and paucity of ideas, is not a very cheering experience for those interested in the simplest standards of good speech. A rapid mumbling and slurring of English syllables characterize the speech of our time. To speak slowly and carefully is considered dull or pedantic.

The microphone has changed the art and craft of speech and oratory. All at once distance has been bridged and persuasiveness contracted to the volume of a whisper. Frequencies have been changed. The value of vowels has been lost in the clatter of consonants. Precision and melody have been sacrificed to the speed of sound. Silence is no longer golden; it is not even a marketable commodity.

Our aim is the clear, audible, and pleasing expression of meaning, but perhaps we have aimed to achieve too much too soon. No one will deny that proper breathing is the foundation of good speech, but how does one teach children how to breathe? Even if one could, is that their most important need?

Why invite young people to practise modulation and rhythm, shading and perspective before they have some

idea of the importance of clear, crisp, and precise enunciation and articulation? Enunciation is the telling out clearly
and distinctly of the syllable or syllables of a word, like
were (wer), *student* (stu-dent), *institution* (in-sti-tu shon), *picturesque* (pic-tu-resk), or *column* (kol um). Articulation is
the uniting, by means of intelligent and appropriate movement of the vocal organs, of the syllables that make up
a word, like *primarily* (pri ma-ri-li), *million* (mil yon), *rhythm*
(rithm), *mischievous* (mis chi-vus), or *amateur* (am a-tur).

To abundant regular practice in enunciation and
articulation add practice in phrasing and emphasis and
watch the pupil's confidence in himself and pride in good
speech develop. These things he can do and should do:
many of the other aims in oral reading are adult activities
for which the pupil has not yet developed what is called
a reading readiness. The tape-recorder at this stage is a
useful instrument for individual instruction.

What accent should be taught and on whose authority?
The pupil should be taught the accent of the thinking
minority (to which the teacher should belong) of the community to which the pupil belongs. Man is master of his
tongue, not its slave. In a rapidly changing world good
taste takes precedence over rules of textbook, language,
grammar, and etiquette.

What models should be used? In oral reading, the sentence is the smallest working unit. Prose should be prefer-
red to poetry or drama, at least at the beginning, so that
attention can be concentrated on the enunciation and
articulation of words and their meanings. There will be
plenty of time later for rhythm and its emotional meaning.
The models should be chosen from the prose of master
craftsmen, writers sensitive to the meaning and power of
words, men and women who have something of value and
interest to say to young people.

Such an example is the following, a passage consisting

of 164 words and quite sufficient in amount for a thirty-minute period of practice in speech and oral reading:

> That man, I think, has had a liberal education who has been so trained in youth that his body is the ready servant of his will, and does with ease and pleasure all the work that as a mechanism, it is capable of; whose intellect is a clear, cold, logic engine, with all its parts of equal strength, and in smooth working order; ready, like a steam engine, to be turned to any kind of work, and spin the gossamers as well as forge the anchors of the mind; whose mind is stored with a knowledge of the great and fundamental truths of Nature and of the laws of her operations; one who, no stunted ascetic, is full of life and fire, but whose passions are trained to come to heel by a vigorous will, the servant of a tender conscience; who has learned to love all beauty, whether of Nature or of art, to hate all vileness, and to respect others as himself.
>
> — Thomas Huxley

This passage contains an essential ingredient for practice in oral reading, namely content worth contemplating. It is all one long sentence and yet it is clear and immediately comprehensible. The reason is that it is well organized on the basis of comparisons. The body is the mechanism, the intellect an engine, the mind a storehouse, and the passions are compared to foxhounds. One clause ends naturally and sensibly with a preposition even as does Juliet's reply to the nurse when she was asked if she wished to wed. "It is an honour that I dream not of." No one would have believed her, had she said *of which I never dream.*

This passage also contains some characteristic English phrases that every student of language (even where Latin is still unknown) should observe. Latin words from the Mediterranean basin commingle effectively with Saxon words from the Baltic basin in phrases like "fundamental truths," "stunted ascetic," "rigorous will," and "spin the gossamers and forge the anchors." This is a condition commonly found in the works of major English writers. Wordsworth speaks of life's "transient sorrows": had he made both words Latin, *transient dolours*, or both Saxon, *passing sorrows*, the delicate effect of his original phrase would have vanished much as the charm vanishes from couples seen too long engaged. It is the euphony of sound and sense that guides the master writer to his choice, not the thumbing of dictionaries. Good taste is the final test of language.

This brings us naturally to silent reading and the study of literature. Here again speed is the demon to divert us from our purpose. Literature provides experience that is duplicated nowhere else in the curriculum. The amount of printed matter available today is beyond the comprehension of anyone to calculate. Consequently the literature that is studied in school and the kind of reading that is cultivated there must be the acknowledged best. It is in school that the foundation of literary and aesthetic taste is laid. There is no time for shoddy matter or method. Excellence is the watchword and touchstone.

We have all seen books, bearing titles like *Tom Sawyer*, *Treasure Island*, or *Lorna Doone*, that are travesties of the original masterpieces, written down to a word count and to an intelligence graded by psychologists or sociologists who pretend to know a great deal about human beings. It is clear that they know nothing about literature or the nature of literary experience. What good is the skeleton of the story without the warm flesh in which it is clothed? The artist who created the characters and incidents also created the imaginary world in which they had their being. The story exists only in the language and in the linguistic patterns of the creative artist.

We have all seen texts that present Shakespeare's teachable dramas in contemporary language. How can the pinnacles of Shakespeare's wide-ranging imagination be reached by wallowing in such bilge? If the pupil is not mature enough to read Shakespeare what benefit is he to derive from Shakespeare's weird incidents and fantastic plots?

We have all seen anthologies of verse in which ingenious editors have replaced a poet's language by their own.

> A poet could not but be gay
> In such a jocund company:

In spite of the editor's zeal to rid us of *jocund*, *merry* fails completely to take its place as Wordsworth well knew and was careful to point out.

We have all seen texts prepared for remedial reading in which little is left to the imagination or the reason. The assumption appears to be based on a desire to nourish the feeble mind on moronic forms and ideas that it may one day find peace with its infirmity.

These are just a few of the crimes against young readers, committed in the name of education by pompous and pragmatic minds. They are cruel jests at the expense of innocent and helpless pupils; and the jesters should not be allowed within speaking distance of the schools.

Almost everything in print goes by the name of literature today. If you wish to find out why one beverage or other detergent is better than another you will be referred to the literature on the subject. Newspapers now advertise their weekly editions as "Complete Week-end Reading for the Whole Family." The task of the teacher of reading is plain to see. Teach for depth of insight rather than for breadth of information, for the nourishing of tastes rather than for the disclosing of talents. Teach the literature of power rather than the literature of opinion; and begin with the pupil rather than with his social environment.

> But here is the finger of God,
>   a flash of the will that can,
> Existent behind all laws,
>   that made them and lo, they are!
> And I know not if, save in this,
>   such gift be allowed to man,
> That out of three sounds he frame,
>   not a fourth sound, but a star.
>
> — Browning: *Abt Vogler*

What applies to the pupil's comprehension also applies to his composition. Reading and writing are the two sides of the same piece of glass. In *How to Read a Book*, Mortimer Adler has this to say:

> If we consider men and women generally, and apart from their professions and occupations, there is only one situation I can think of in which they almost pull themselves up by their bootstraps, making an effort to read better than they usually do. When they are in love and are reading a love letter, they read for all they are worth. They read every word three ways; they read between the lines and in the margins; they read the whole in terms of the parts, and each part in terms of the whole; they grow sensitive to context and ambiguity, to insinuation and implication; they perceive the colour of words, the colour of phrases, and the weight of sentences. They may even take the punctuation into account. Then, if never before or after, they read.

This, you may say, is an anomaly impossible to reproduce in the classroom, but something akin to it can be achieved by skilful questioning and a teacher's enthusiasm for what he is doing. Pupils can be led a long way to see and hear and feel and imagine what the author originally experienced. Here, for example, is an excellent passage of first-class prose:

But although safety first is the rule when tiger-shark are about in numbers, plenty of Gilbertese are ready to fight a lone prowler in its own element. Owing to his great girth, a tiger cannot turn quickly; once launched on its attack, it thunders straight forward like a bull; there lies the hunter's advantage in single combat. Out sailing with a Tarawa friend one day, I pointed out a cruising dorsal fin. 'That's a tababa,' he said 'watch me kill him.'

We lowered sail and drifted. He slid overboard with his knife and paddled around waiting to be noticed. He soon was. The fin began to circle him, and he knew he was being stalked; he trod water; it closed in gradually, lazily to fifteen yards.

He held his knife right-handed, blade down, the handle just above the water, his crooked right elbow pointed always towards the gliding fin. He would have a split second to act in when the charge came. It came from ten yards' range. There was a frothing swirl; the fin shot forward like an arrow; the head and shoulders of the brute broke surface, rolling as they lunged. My friend flicked aside in the last blink of time and shot his knife into the upswinging belly as it surged by. His enemy's momentum did the rest. I saw the belly rip itself open like a zipfastener, discharging blood and guts. The tiger disappeared for a while, to float up dead a hundred yards off.

That kind of single combat used to be fairly common. It was rather like a nice score of fifty at cricket in England; the villagers applauded but did not make a great song about it.

— Arthur Grimble; *A Pattern of Islands.*

Observing the third paragraph; how did he hold his knife? (Do not admit a diagram or an illustration; make words tell the story.) How did he point his elbow? Why? How was he able to do this? Why must he do this? Why is this sentence structure appropriate? Which are the telling words in sentence 4? Why is this structure used? What is the grammatical relationship of "rolling" etc.? Why *flicked* rather than jumped; *blink* rather than second; *upswinging* rather than rising; *surged* rather than passed? How did the author help us to experience the thrill of a close and dangerous contest? This is the product of an alert, sensitive, and perceptive mind. The material is so organized and the words so carefully chosen that the reader's comprehension of the action is made easy.

This practice might be called, for want of a better term, sighted reading — the awakening of response to images, feelings, and ideas. Now observe a few examples of what might be called insighted reading.

> A little water clears us of this deed:
> How easy is it then!

Had Lady Macbeth known of the long history of hand-washing in man's recorded experience, she might have persuaded Shakespeare to spare her the uttering of these revealing words. They strip her conscience of everything but its nakedness. To clarify the significance of one thing, however, a teacher needs to know a great many. Not that he is expected to use hand-washing as a spring board for a plunge into sermonizing: a passing reference or an example will suffice to stir the imaginations and the emotions of a class, and to deepen the irony and the pathos of this dramatic crisis.

> O proper stuff!
> This is the very painting of your fear;
> This is the air-drawn dagger which, you said,
> Led you to Duncan.

The most revealing words in Lady Macbeth's bitter denunciation of Macbeth's behaviour here are "which, you said." When had they discussed this matter? It is not revealed in the play itself. And what had prompted the discussion? Had he been trying to defend, excuse, or explain himself? What did she hope to gain by challenging him with it here? It provides, at least, a profound insight into the relation of these two creatures to each other. In Shakespeare the little words are often laden with intended meaning.

The strings, my lord, are false.

When the dreaming Lucius unwittingly dropped these words into the main cacophony of *Julius Caesar,* where everyone else is screaming with a lust for power, he made an ironic comment on the nature of the whole play. The words fall shrewdly to the purpose.

These are examples of insights available to secondary school teachers and pupils in their daily work. The study of mathematics and science is likewise alive with insights into the problems of human existence. A lesson in simple interest, for example, might very well lead to fresh insights into the profit motive. The practice, however, requires of the teacher both creative and critical thinking.

The intelligent reading of words and numbers is a key to learning, and learning leads to the discernment of significances. Every lesson should have its telescopic vision as well as its microscopic view: both should be concomitant in education. Unless important facts are presented in large perspective, related to life, and made integral parts of a pupil's mental furnishings, they are soon forgotten, and should be. Knowledge is informative when it creates or satisfies a need, and the school exists to provide proper inducements for the searching out of such insights as will give meaning essential to useful learning. One flash of insight is worth more than hours of drill.

What does all this mean for the pupil? Why is he in school? Many people would claim that he is there to form character; others, to acquire useful knowledge; others, to learn a skill; and still others, to keep out of the weather. In the light of what has already been said, the pupil is in school primarily to develop his mental faculties, to learn to think for himself, and to use his intellect, as the creative artist does, to clarify and give meaning to his experience. He is in school to turn a cold and impartial chaos into a warm personal cosmos, and to enlarge the unique world of his own total personality.

As a result of his pursuit of ideas and insights, the pupil in the secondary school may become more mature in judgment and more refined in tastes. He may even gather to himself a set of values. If his interest in learning and in thinking creatively is genuinely awakened, his studies may become not a labour, but a personal satisfaction in achievement. This is by no means the only concern of good teachers everywhere, but it is the most important and lasting of the pupil's accomplishments.

Teach, then, for experience, not appreciation; for vision, not alone for view! Teach the work of master writers, not the conceits of nonentities! And your pupils may one day rise up and call you blessed! You will have taught them to discriminate between art and propaganda, and to read and write creatively and speak correctly.

IV

Teaching Patterns

Reporters, covering a recent symposium on *Modern Man: Master or Slave,* picked up some refreshing ideas for our consumption. "Within the next ten years," they reported "the book as we know it today will begin to disappear. Books are cumbersome, expensive, impractical, and they gather dust." Books in the future will be produced "in the form of pellets and everyone will carry around a little machine to magnify these pellets." "The function of an author will be replaced by a computer." "Already it has been shown that computer poetry was difficult to distinguish from much original modern poetry." Henceforth books as we know them will be found not in libraries, but in museums. What is to become of the teachers was not made clear, but before we divert our pensions and reserve berths in the local temples of the muses, contemplate the marvels of the world we will be leaving behind.

Can we not hear the pupil protesting that he picked up the wrong pellets or that he swallowed them whole, or that his computer was out of order? Can we not see the parent's face when he discovers on his child's report card that success depends on more and better computation, or the noncomputability of your son disrupts the class? Can we not feel for the teacher when forty computers begin buzzing away in different keys all around him? One may ask, sympathetically, of course, if the teacher has had his pellets today?

Wiseacres have proclaimed that Shakespeare cannot happen again. All that is now necessary is the reconstruction of the Globe theatre to house a good computer well-fed with historical records and old wives' tales for the production of all the dramas that Stratford can produce in the next one hundred years. So long as Niagara continues to deliver power, smart computers will be able to flush and retrieve Shakespearean sonnets from boudoirs where dark ladies are retired.

Given a plum tree in an English garden, a nightingale to nest nearby, a properly attuned computer to record the song, and *Odes to a Nightingale* can become as plentiful as Falstaff's reasons for preferring sack to pickled herring. And imagine what would happen if some bluejays came screaming in from a nearby meadow. When a computer has created a character as inimitable as that of Falstaff's, the need will already have come for us to join the collection of curiosities in a museum of natural history. Until then, however, we had better console ourselves by contemplating the mysterious behaviour of the human spirit and its endless variety.

Nothing is so composing to the spirit as the creative act of composition, the act of making something that did not heretofore exist. Whether the carpenter of Nazareth was concerned with the form and shaping of a yoke or the point and purpose of a parable, the creation of something harmonious and useful and acceptable must have lightened His spirit immeasurably. Sir Winston Churchill reported that, when during the Second World War he was called upon to form a government, he went home and slept soundly all night, secure apparently in the belief that he at last held the power to frame the epic of victory and that he could lead the British people to accept him as the poet of their salvation.

Every normal human being has within him the capacity for creation, and provided he discovers the proper tools for the exercise of his peculiar personal trade or talents, he can achieve a self-realization and fulfilment without parallel in the world. Whether he works with his hands or his head, the mind of a maker, i.e. the poet, the painter, the composer, the architect, or the artisan, is always present in the backroom directing the show. No matter what he teaches, the teacher, too, is a maker, an architect of human accomplishment. He is busy every day helping young people to discover their potential, the singular gifts by which they can make a contribution and bring a little more harmony into the complicated scheme of things.

This is a fact long overlooked by policy makers in education. The blind worship of knowledge or skill for its own sake bedeviled the system for more than a century. Reliance on knowledge without understanding and on skill without zeal and personal involvement has kept alive the great deception, the function perfunctory. Of what value is the accumulation of knowledge if the latent talents of the pupil, his initiative and imagination, his individual spirit remain uncommitted and unreleased?

Community colleges, freed from the domination of the universities may lead to the rapid emancipation of the secondary schools from the despotism of intellectual snobbery and the mediaeval concepts cherished by the committee of Ontario University Presidents. Freed from the curse of these tyrannies, the secondary schools will be able to serve more accurately and effectively the needs of their communities and their pupils. No matter what course the pupil follows, technical, commercial, academic or social, he will need brains, that is initiative and imagination, to succeed. Success here means the personal realization of the best achievement of which he is capable at the lathe or in the language, and the two skills are closely related.

In the study of poetry he may discover new ideas, new

insights, fresh language, and the imaginative patterns that contain them. He may perceive how masterpieces are created as harmonious wholes made of many interrelated parts, and how excellence is achieved. He may discover that a Shakespearean drama or a lyric by Emily Dickinson is not confining, restrictive, and dogmatic, but rather open at both ends and forever radiating more and more meaning. He may, indeed, trace the path by which genius has found release for pent-up feelings. Likewise in mathematics, science, music, painting, carpentry, and in any other "putting together of things connected but whose connection has just been seen," he may tread in imagination the same steps originally taken by the greatest makers, builders, and composers. Education thence becomes something lived through rather than learned about. All artificial rivalries and petty jealousies among so-called departments of learning disappear. The individual in his relationship to his environment, self-realizing and self-sacrificing, holds the centre of the educational stage. How composing to the spirit is the harmonizing of internal conflicts, either by original creation or by the recreation of the achievements of others! And how aimless, dispossessed, and delinquent is life lived without this modicum of human dignity!

Sixty years ago in an attempt to outwit an examiner, I memorized whole paragraphs of Caesar's *Gallic Wars* with their appropriate translations. No one ever explained the whys and wherefores of Caesar's epistles. I learned them by heart, believing, I suppose, that one day I would know a lot of what was considered by some remote authorities the best things to know. Thirty years ago I found a small book entitled *Julius Caesar* by John Buchan that explained the whole business and could have given point and purpose to my study. I mention this merely to show the difference between meaningless learning and what might have been for me at least an experience in living mentally.

The mind today, thanks to satellites and computers,

and hundreds of other ingenious devices, is confounded by a world unlike anything that has gone before. New values and new concepts are projecting the mind out to the brink of new decisions. Much of what has passed for the content of education may have to be discarded and new attitudes created to help man adjust intelligently and imaginatively to the new predicament in which he finds himself. The literature of chronological sequences, like Tennyson's *Enoch Arden* and *The Brook*, the unchallenging progression of events from "and then" "and then" to "and then" "and then" has already given place to the literature of ideas and consequences. What poetry shall we teach? The answer is the poetry of ideas whether they be the insights of Chaucer or the reflections of Earle Birney, remembering all the while that what the poet is revealing are *tentatives*, not *tenets*. The poet begins somewhere and leaves off elsewhere, and he is never true to himself when he is opinionated and dogmatic. In a tenetless world people are searching for tentatives to live by, and the modern poet is well equipped to help them, teachers and pupils alike, in their quest.

The saddest man alive is he who cannot adjust quickly to new ways of looking at old truths. Believing that the narrow world of his hard-won but inherited convictions will never pass away, he is content to abide in the secure shelter of outworn opinions. The poet, if he is permitted to speak, can cure him of his mental ills. Where else but in poetry can he find the mental freshness and vigourous thrusts of thought, the vibrant imagery, the dynamic language, and the feeling for rhythmical cadences? Where else can he find what Wordsworth called the "authentic tidings of invisible things"? Where else can he become aware of the lights and shadows within his own mind? Emerson, weathering the climate of another day, observed "Every spirit makes its house, but afterwards the house confines the spirit." Contemporary man, on the other hand, is on the march with space as his horizon and fluctuating visions to light him on his way. In the van may be found the inventors and the poets. Poetry is concerned with some of the profoundest and most critical issues that confront the human spirit, and good poetry, in spite of the computers, remains both our richest heritage and our inspiring hope, an open highway of imaginative experience. These random thoughts on the importance of poetry lead naturally to some reflections on how it may be taught, and these in turn lead to the substance of poetry itself.

Structure alone, however, will not guarantee a literary masterpiece as will be shown by a comparison of Keats' *On First Looking into Chapman's Homer* (1816) with Andrew Lang's *The Odyssey* (1879):

On First Looking into Chapman's Homer

Much have I travelled in the realms of gold,
    And many goodly states and kingdoms seen;
    Round many western islands have I been
Which bards in fealty to Apollo hold.
Oft of one wide expanse had I been told
    That deep-browed Homer ruled as his demesne;
    Yet did I never breathe its pure serene
Till I heard Chapman speak out loud and bold;
Then felt I like some watcher of the skies
    When a new planet swims into his ken;
Or like stout Cortez when with eagle eyes
    He stared at the Pacific — and all his men
Looked at each other with a wild surmise —
    Silent, upon a peak in Darien.

                                        –Keats

The Odyssey

As one that for a weary space has lain
    Lulled by the song of Circe and her wine
    In gardens near the pale of Proserpine,

Where that Aegean isle forgets the main,
And only the low lutes of lore complain,
  And only shadows of wan lovers pine,
    As such an one were glad to know the brine
Salt on his lips, and the large air again, –
So gladly from the songs of modern speech
  Men turn, and see the stars, and feel the free
Shrill wind beyond the close of heavy flowers,
  And, through the music of the languid hours,
They hear like ocean on a western beach
  The surge and thunder of the Odyssey.

– Lang

In the first, every metaphor and simile, every image and allusion is consistent and poetic, and the rhythms lift the whole comparison to an imaginative plane where beauty, truth, and excellence are enshrined. In the second, only the last line

The surge and thunder of the Odyssey

reveals that a poet may have passed this way.

As one that for a weary space has lain

is an inept and awkward beginning. The images and allusions are forced and ineffectual. "Low lutes of lore," "wan lovers pine," "songs of modern speech," and "music of the languid hours" are vague, unhappy, and unconvincing phrases that belong somewhere "beyond the close of heavy flowers." In form and subject these two passages are alike, but the first is poetry and the second is laboured verse.

And what, you may ask, does all this mean for the teacher? It means that he should not allow a poem to disintegrate in his hands by going over it again and again like a squirrel on a treadmill, once for theme, once for form, once for rhyme scheme, once for rhythms, once for metaphors, once for diction, and finally once more for utter boredom. At all costs, he should preserve the interrelation of form and content. The only worthy meaning a simile can have is discovered in its context. Even a title is meaningless detached from the theme it entitles.

This is an old, old story, but it needs repeating again and again. Only last year an American text advocated the same squirrel-in-a-cage method recommended twenty years ago at the University of London School of Education. It is apparent that people who lack the tenacity of purpose to pursue meaning to its lair often amaze themselves and exhaust their pupils by collecting and naming the parts of poetry, by dabbling in biographical and historical details, and by comparison of themes and forms. The teacher must forever be alert to the difference between wholes and parts, between real education and mere erudition, and alive to the distinction in meaning between the infinitives *educare,* meaning to nurture and nourish, and *educere,* meaning to lead out and elicit.

What poetry should be taught? That which each individual teacher of poetry believes to be genuine material for his own pupils.

Why should it be taught? That each individual teacher may test for himself his belief that particular poets have something of value for his particular pupils.

How should it be taught? In such a way that each individual teacher may discover the reach of his pupil's imaginations on their way to mental maturity and serenity of spirit.

And what, it may be asked, have these objectives to do with educational researchers, statisticians, and computers?

V

Points of View

The following trials and tracings in the art of teaching are recordings of actual lesson outlines. For beginners they may suggest ways of arousing and sustaining interest. They are neither models nor guidelines, but mere intimations concerning meaning and method as both are perceived and practised by one teacher. Only a stupid or pretentious person would attempt to apply them pragmatically as if they were his own. Every teacher frames and draws his own response from each particular class, and that response is not fixed but flexible. A teacher must have a plan and a clear idea where the plan is leading, but he should be ready to shift his tactics on the instant as the class pursues the changing course of its investigation. It is the surprise of the unexpected that makes the art of teaching a continually challenging activity.

From time to time the question is asked: Should poetry be analysed? The inference is, of course, that it should not be analysed. The dissected flower lies strewn on the grass, devoid of form, rhythm, or beauty. The assumption that a poem analysed may suffer a similar fate, is false. Flower and poem belong to different worlds, the one blooms for a season and dies, the other blooms in all seasons and lives.

Ely Cathedral is a poem in stone. An ordinary observer

may be impressed by its immensity. Guided and instructed, however, by an architect familiar with the design, the observer is likely to carry away in the packsack of his memory a recollection of artistic magnificence, and the wonder of superb human achievement. The analogy between the architect and the teacher is not far-fetched. The chief function of the teacher of literature is, likewise, to awaken response, nourish the mind, and stimulate the imagination. He builds not in stone, but in ideas moulded by the various responses awakened. When the pupil and the poet meet on equal terms, they share in an experience. The teacher as artist provides the background harmony.

Critics may dismiss some of the answers attributed to pupils as unreal. They are, of course, composite answers that sum up a variety of responses, and they are presented in this form to conserve space and facilitate sequential reading. After all, the lesson-patterns that follow are not intended to be definitive or dogmatic. They are merely suggestions concerning the ways and means by which others may be led to apprehend literary experience.

Another aim of the teacher is to provide his students with abundant opportunities for decision-making. Surely there is nothing either mechanical or passive in the students' exercise of their mental faculties within the language and structure set down by the poet!

1. *The Twa Corbies*

In 1814 Sir Walter Scott published *Waverley,* the first in a series of novels, or historical romances. Previous to this date he had published three longer poems that became famous in his time, *The Lady of the Lake* in 1810, *Marmion* in 1808, and *The Lay of the Last Minstrel* in 1805. These are all important events in the life of a professional literary man, but an event that may in the light of literary history prove more significant is the fact that in 1802 he published in three volumes *The Minstrelsy of the Scottish Border*. With the exception of two short translations this was Scott's first venture into the field of literature.

As a young man in his late twenties he tramped about the border country between Scotland and England collecting whatever stories in verse old men and women cared to recite to him. His little red notebook became a familiar sight as he stood by cottage doors or sat by fireplaces. The zeal of this literary antiquarian soon fired the imaginations and revived the memories of many people who were genuinely interested in helping Scott with his collection. A man named Robertson, for instance, recited for Scott one day the poem we are about to read. How fortunate for the millions of readers who have since taken delight in the ancient popular ballads that Scott had the foresight and wisdom to collect when he did.

After an oral reading of the poem by the teacher, the pupils read silently, clearing the meanings of all difficult or strange words and phrases by reference to the glossary and notes in the text. Then one or two pupils may volunteer to read the poem aloud.

The Twa Corbies

As I was walking all alane,
I heard two corbies making a mane;
The tane unto the t'other say,
"Whar sall we gang and dine to-day?"

"In behint yon auld fail dyke,
I wot there lies a new-slain knight;
And naebody kens that he lies there,
But his hawk, his hound, and lady fair.

"His hound is to the hunting gane,
His hawk to fetch the wild-fowl hame,
His lady's ta'en another mate,
So we may mak our dinner sweet.

"Ye'll sit on his white hause-bane,
And I'll pike out his bonny blue eyne:
Wi' ae lock o' his gowden hair,
We'll theek our nest when it grows bare.

"Mony a one for him makes mane,
But nane sall ken whar he is gane;
O'er his white banes, when they are bare,
The wind sall blaw for evermair."
                                    – Anonymous

T.   Why does this poem interest you?

P.   It tells a story of death and mystery with clues suggestive of foul play.

P.   The ideas, images, and language tell of social life and customs long since passed away.

P.   The confirmed beat of the rhythm helps to convince us that this was a personal experience, and that the incident really happened.

T.   Who is the speaker?

P.   A big black crow.

T.   Read the first stanza aloud, and try again please.

P.   The speaker is some person who heard two crows talking to each other.

T.   What do we learn concerning the interests of the speaker?

P.   He must have been a bird-watcher who liked to walk alone.

P.   Either he understood the language of crows or his imagination was very lively.

P.   He liked morbid stories with plenty of gruesome details.

T.   What would have been lost, had the poem begun with this couplet?

> Twa corbies sat upon a tree
> And croaked a tale full jocundly.

P. The story would not have been told as a personal experience, and consequently would have lost some of its impressiveness.

T. What would have been lost, had the first stanza ended with this line:

> Whar sall we find a meal today?

P. This plain matter-of-fact question would not have conveyed the impression of a formal festive occasion as may be inferred from "gang" and "dine."

T. Why is this a good opening stanza?

P. It sets the stage, introduces the characters, and opens the plot.

P. It projects the reader directly into the scene without wasting time preparing him for the story.

T. The first corby asks an important question, and the remainder of the poem is taken up with the second corby's reply. What story does he tell?

P. It is a story of unfaithfulness and desertion. A young knight who is apparently a popular figure in the community meets death in a manner that arouses many suspicions.

T. How is the story told?

P. Only the bare and macabre details of the dramatic incidents are given. A good deal of characterization is suggested. A regular rhythm and a fast moving series of rhyming couplets reinforce the realism and the overtones of parable. It sounds like a true story.

T. Which receives the greater emphasis in the telling — death or desertion?

P. The death of the knight is accepted as a fact in the course of natural events; the story is more concerned with the suggestions of desertion and foul play.

> "In behint yon auld fail dyke,
>   I wot there lies a new-slain knight;
>   And naebody kens that he lies there,
>   But his hawk, his hound, and lady fair.

> "His hound is to the hunting gane,
>   His hawk to fetch the wild-fowl hame,
>   His lady's ta'en another mate,
>   So we may mak our dinner sweet."

T. Why is "yon" the most telling word in the first line?

P. It suggests that this place was near at hand and familiar to both corbies. Perhaps a favourite haunt into which people seldom ventured.

T. Which is the most revealing word in the second line?

P. The fact that the knight is "new-slain", the body still warm perhaps, is offered as good reason why both corbies could look forward to a delectable feast undisturbed by intruders.

T. How did this corby know so much about this event?

P. He may have observed the incident.

P. As a bird of ill omen he may have more than normal sight and insight. He certainly does not respect other creatures, or even human beings, very much.

T. There is here a suggestion of a gradation of faithlessness. A Knight was usually mounted on a horse and attended by a squire. Neither is mentioned here. I wonder why these particular facts are given, while others are omitted?

P. They may suggest something of the character and preoccupation of this young man. Loyalties, at any rate, were quickly changed.

> "Ye'll sit on his white hause-bane,
> And I'll pike out his bonny blue eyne:
> Wi' ae lock o' his gowden hair,
> We'll theek our nest when it grows bare."

T. What makes these details so ghoulish?

P. The corby regards this once handsome, golden-haired, and blue-eyed youth as no more than an occasion for a sumptuous feast.

P. He suggests a division of labour and desserts. The connotations of the word "pike" are gruesome enough!

T. Another version of this ballad reads:

> "We'll theek our nest when it's a' blawn bare."

Which version do you prefer? Discussion.

P.
> "Mony a one for him makes mane,
> But nane sall ken whar he is gane;
> O'er his white banes, when they are bare,
> The wind sall blaw for evermair."

T. References are made to moaning in both the first and the last stanzas. What is the difference between the two meanings?

P. In the first stanza the corbies are lamenting their empty stomachs; in the last, people are mourning the loss of a knight. The one is physical, the other mental.

T. Again some kind of occult prescience is attributed to the corby. He appears to know a good deal about the affairs of human beings. In the last line he appears to be expressing delight at human misfortune. How can you account for this?

P. The corbies, as creatures of nature, may be exultant over human nature. This note is often sounded in the ancient popular ballad, as it is in *Sir Patrick Spens* and in the modern "artistic" ballad, *Rosabelle*. In some respects nature triumphant over human nature was a traditional theme.

T. Under what circumstances do you suppose this ballad was heard in early times?

P. Perhaps a minstrel chanted it on a village common or before assembled knights and ladies in a baron's banquet hall.

T. Why did he bother to remember and recite this particular story?

P. Presumably his audience would approve of it and enjoy even the warnings it contains.

T. If our early, listening ancestors liked this kind of story, what is reflected here of their tastes, literary and otherwise?

P. Apparently they did not waste time sentimentalizing over death. Death and forgetfulness were among life's commonplaces, and inevitable.

P   The things of this earth were regarded as fleeting, impermanent, and evanescent.

P. They took delight in the grim, the gruesome, and the cynical. The stark undertones of treachery and tragedy stirred their imaginations. They appear callous, cruel, and blunt.

P   Their emotions were concerned with both the elemental and the temporal. People in trouble, especially knights and ladies, interested them.

P. Dialogue, even between creatures to which they could attribute human qualities, appealed to them.

T. How does this ballad compare with some contemporary songs, commonly called ballads, and heard on the radio today? Discussion.

T.   Dr. E.M.W. Tillyard, the English scholar and critic, once classified poetry as direct or oblique. Which is this?

P.   This ballad appears, on first reading, to be direct and complete, but presently so many important facts are found missing, so many details are fragmentary, that the poem becomes much less than straightforward and is far from being conclusive.

T.   Why is it, nevertheless, called poetry?

P.   This ballad interests me because it reads like a fable, uses a number of clear, hard details, presents a realistic view of life, and yet leaves much to the imagination. I can now understand why it is popular with many readers and why it is a part of our literary heritage.

T.   Certainly when compared with *The Three Ravens, The Twa Corbies* is distinctly a literary masterpiece, cast in a vertical pattern rather than a horizontal plane. *The Three Ravens* tells a tragic story of a knight whose hounds, hawks, and wife remained faithful at his death. In the ballad they are all commended for their loyalty, the knight's body is buried by his widow, and the three hungry ravens go without their breakfast. There is little here to excite the imagination or awaken the sense of wonder. Instead of pathos obliquely cultivated we have a pathetic narrative uncharged with anything but its own recital.

The Three Ravens

There were three ravens sat on a tre,
They were as blacke as they might be:

The one of them said to his mate,
"Where shall we our breakfast take?"

"Downe in yonder greene field,
There lies a knight slain under his shield;

"His hounds they lie downe at his feete,
  So well they their master keepe;

"His haukes they flie so eagerlie,
  There's no fowle dare come him nie.

"Down there comes a fallow doe,
  As great with yong as she might goe,

"She lift up his bloudy hed,
  And kist his wounds that were so red.

"She got him up upon her backe,
  And carried him to earthen lake.

"She buried him before the prime,
  She was dead her self ere even song time.

"God send every gentleman,
  Such haukes, such houndes, and such a leman."

Method on Twa Corbies

1. Presents historical basis of its discovery!

2. Reflects an oral literary tradition that is still alive!

3. Recommends the use of variants!

4. Emphasizes the importance of decision-making as an adjunct to learning!

5. Experience is given priority over appreciation.

6. The parts of the poem are reconstructed into a whole of parts.

7. Stanzas are read aloud as study progresses.

8. This lesson analysis is not presented with a view to encourage slavish imitation by others. It aims chiefly to illustrate the importance of sequential questioning and the need to keep attention fixed on the central theme of the poem. No two teachers will approach their subject in the same way. The pupils in a class,

moreover, will not all, it is hoped, express the same responses. Each one will take away from the study his own literary experience. Its acquisition is a very personal matter.

9. The opinion of a literary critic, discreetly introduced, can be a useful aid to teaching.

10. In teaching such a poem as this, it is well worthwhile today to ask the question, Is this poetry?

11. The comparison of the two different treatments of the same basic material illustrates very well the difference between the vertical pattern and the horizontal plane, between what is a work of art and what is not.

2. *How Sweet I Roamed*

Poets often use a simple means to express a profound idea. William Blake, speculating on the fate of man in this earthly predicament, turned to lyric verse to express his feelings.

How Sweet I Roamed

How sweet I roamed from field to field,
  And tasted all the summer's pride,
Till I the Prince of Love beheld
  Who in the sunny beams did glide!

He showed me lilies for my hair,
  And blushing roses for my brow;
He led me through his gardens fair
  Where all his golden pleasures grow.

With sweet May-dews my wings were wet,
  And Phoebus fired my vocal rage;
He caught me in his silken net,
  And shut me in his golden cage.

> He loves to sit and hear me sing;
>   Then, laughing, sports and plays with me;
> Then stretches out my golden wing,
>   And mocks my loss of liberty.
>   — William Blake

(The poem is read aloud by the teacher, and then by several pupils)

T.   To what does the poet compare himself?

P.   To a bird in a cage.

T.   Why does he feel this way?

P.   He has lost his freedom of action. He feels cabin'd, cribb'd, confin'd.

T.   How is it that he is so conscious of his "loss of liberty"?

P.   He was once free.

> How sweet I roamed from field to field,
>   And tasted all the summer's pride,
> Till I the Prince of Love beheld
>   Who in the sunny beams did glide!

T.   What made his first state of existence so sweet?

P.   He was free to rove, ramble, or wander about the earth as he pleased, to come and go when he wished.

P.   "Roamed" suggests that the poet was free to wander at will because he had no cares or duties to restrict his activities. He could roam for the sake of roaming.

T.   Why is "tasted" a more telling word in this context than *sampled* or *partook of*?

P.   "Tasted" suggests that he put summer's excellence to the test. He had a nice perception and could discern what was worth savouring. He liked whate'er he looked on and his looks went everywhere among the choicest pleasures that summer had to offer. His freedom tasted sweet as he moved about from flower to flower like a humming-bird or a goldfinch.

T. What put an end to his freedom?

P. He met the Prince of Love and succumbed to his charms.

T. Where did he encounter this gallant?

P. He "beheld" him riding in a sunbeam, the very symbol of light that pervades the universe.

T. Why is "beheld" a more telling word than *observed* in this context?

P. "Beheld" suggests that he was confronted suddenly by the Prince of Love *gliding* in a stream of light. The poet discovered him by a *flash of insight,* as if he had unexpectedly apprehended and comprehended the significance of the Prince.

T. Why is the form appropriate to the thought here expressed?

P. The rhythm and the rhymes are light and lilting and well suited to the faery images and ideas of the poem.

P. This is the simplest of lyric verse forms.

T. Who is the "He" referred to in the next stanza?

P. The Prince of Love becomes the master of ceremonies. He is in control, and the "I" of stanza one is reduced to "me" in the remainder of the poem as he succumbs to his master.

> He showed me lilies for my hair,
>   And blushing roses for my brow;
> He led me through his gardens fair
>   Where all his golden pleasures grow.

T. What other contrasts are evident between the second stanza and the first?

P.   Instead of roaming freely as he wished, he is now "led" about and shown what he should see. He is given lilies (symbols of purity) and roses (symbols of love). He is led into a veritable Garden of Eden where everything is "golden" rather than "sunny," and artfully cultivated rather than natural and variable.

P.   In the third stanza May-dews, like spring rain, suggest that he is confined to a state of perpetual youth.

P.   Phoebus, the god of light and song and music, lent the fire of his inspiration to force the poet to the height of his poetic power. No longer is the poet free to sing as he pleases.

P.   Without warning he is caught up harshly in a fowler's net and shut up firmly in a cage.

P.   But that is not all. In the last stanza he is humiliated. His golden wing is classified with an artificial golden cage and golden pleasures in the Prince of Love's conventions. His behaviour is subject to imitation and mimicry. He no longer can spread his wing: it is stretched for him. He is laughed at contemptuously for having lost his liberty. The "silken net" in which he was caught may have been made of sky-like filament; hence, there may be a suggestion of deception intended.

T.   The poet's spirit is compared to a beautiful bird with a beautiful song made captive by its own desire. The very pride and pleasure it enjoyed became the bars of its prisoner's cage. What has the poet been trying to say in this poem?

P.   The poem may be interpreted at various depths or heights below or above the patent level of a song-bird confined to a cage or the contemplation of mythological "gardens" that one enters at his peril. The poet may have been suggesting that our passions make prisoners of us all.

P. Perhaps he wished to point out the irony of our situation that even when confined we still have our desires to plague us.

P. It may be that the poet wished to comment on our predicament as creatures of the creator. Licence and liberty are different ideas, and individual freedom depends for its existence upon the acceptance of certain restrictions. Blake's mood is one of acceptance rather than self-pity. It is by driving hard against the bars that great things are achieved.

T. How well has the poet succeeded in expressing this meaning?

P. In form this lyric is as simple as a nursery rhyme.

P. The imagery is clear-cut, sharp, and bright. Every statement is firm and precise, like the lines of an etcher or an engraver.

P. The poem, nevertheless, is built in a vertical pattern with every item in its proper place to send the mind rocketing to different heights of meaning.

T. If this poem may be accepted as a delightful observation on so profound a theme as the nature and dimensions of man's freedom, it is worth including in the treasure of memory. Let us repeat it in concert until we have made it our own.

A Few Notes on Method

The adult mind often jumps to conclusions. Frequently it is wrong; sometimes it is right, but right or wrong it is difficult for another mind to accept the verdict without supporting evidence. Someone may dismiss Blake's poem as a reflection of the poet's courage, of his restrictions rather than of his convictions, without attempting to verify the deduction. Unless the meaning can be verified by reference to all the facts of the poem, it is not the meaning of the poem. The search for truth is a systematic pursuit that ends in the accumulation of many minor decisions. In the classroom the method of approach is almost as important as the matter sought.

The historian of literary conventions may feel that a valuable opportunity has here been missed to explore Greek mythology or mediaeval philosophy. The golden pleasures of perilous gardens can be appreciated without reference to Chaucer or Spenser. Blake's problem is not like Spenser's. Better than an excursion in "The Faerie Queene," would be a longer sojourn with Blake himself. "The Echoing Green," for example, presents the little joys of man's allotted years.

Biography is often interesting and sometimes indispensable to the literary student. The teacher's difficulty is in keeping it under control, and in choosing essential facts that illuminate the subject under discussion. Much talk about Blake's aptitude as an illustrator and engraver might easily lead the mind far away from the central theme of this poem. Good teaching is marked chiefly by the pursuit of insights, not information, and insights appear at different levels of interest rather than at different distances from one another. A poem is a whole made up of many parts, and every part is essential to the whole. Gyration of thought may produce saturation of feeling.

3. *Spring and Fall*

T. Sprung rhythm, as practised by Gerard Manley Hopkins, requires that the lines of a poem have the same number of stressed syllables with varying numbers of unstressed syllables. As I read aloud the following poem which has four stresses in every line you may suspect that you are about to observe the artificiality of form and the absence of meaning. Quite the opposite is true. The stresses reinforce the meaning, and make the matter and the method inseparable.

Spring and Fall
To a Young Child

Margaret, are you grieving
Over Goldengrove unleaving?
Leaves, like the things of man, you
With your fresh thoughts care for, can you?
Ah! as the heart grows older
It will come to such sights colder
By and by, nor spare a sigh
Though worlds of wanwood leafmeal lie;
And yet you will weep and know why.
Now no matter, child, the name;
Sorrow's springs are the same.
Nor mouth had, no nor mind, expressed
What heart heard of, ghost guessed:
It is the blight man was born for,
It is Margaret you mourn for.

           – Gerard Manley Hopkins

Now read the poem silently, placing the emphasis where you think it should be in each line.
    What is the central image of this poem?

P.   The poet observes a "young child" in a sorrowful mood. She is grieving, he supposes, at the falling of autumn leaves, and he interprets her feelings in the light of his own experience.

T.   Margaret, are you grieving
        Over Goldengrove unleaving?

What advantages has this phrasing over a paraphrase such as *Because a grove of trees is shedding its golden leaves?* Is that why you are grieving, Margaret?

P.   "Goldengrove" is a striking and picturesque way of suggesting to the imagination a grove of trees in their autumn glory.

P. "Unleaving" implies that the leaves possess the power to detach themselves at will and go.

P. "Over" is a much more revealing word than *because* in this context. Margaret is grieving *over* them, not because of them.

T. What new ideas are presented in the second question?

P.   Leaves, like the things of man, you
          With your fresh thoughts care for, can you?

The poet is surprised that a child should be concerned with such things. Her "fresh thoughts" should be concerned with spring and young growth rather than with death and decay. Children normally think (care for) little about life's means and ends. The question form points up the irony of the situation.

T. How now does he reflect upon her behaviour? Please read aloud the next five lines.

          Ah! as the heart grows older
          It will come to such sights colder
          By and by, nor spare a sigh
          Though worlds of wanwood leafmeal lie;
          And yet you will weep and know why.

As she grows older, she will see sadder sights than that of falling leaves and remain undisturbed. Though the colourless foliage (wanwood) falls, leaf by leaf or piecemeal (leafmeal), both general and deep (worlds of wanwood), she will not notice (spare a sigh), being completely absorbed with serious human sorrows. She will be old enough to feel personal loss, and to weep in earnest and knowingly. The suggestion is apparent that the poet thinks that she does not now know why she feels sad, that she is grieving intuitively.

P. "You will weep" suggests that she will, when older, have personal experience of grief and will be resolved to weep because she cannot help herself and because it will be the only relief available, grief being the lot of mortal man.

T. What is suggested by the sound and rhythm of the line

> Though worlds of wanwood leafmeal lie?

P. The alliteration and the interplay of vowels make the line run smoothly and at depth. The image is one of leaves piled one upon another to great depth.

T.
> Now no matter, child, the name:
> Sorrow's springs are the same.

What is the "name" he withholds from her? And why does he not mention it?

P. Since the life of man, like that of leaves, ends in death, there is little point in belabouring a fact that he feels that she has discovered intuitively.

T. The next couplet

> Nor mouth had, no nor mind, expressed
> What heart heard of, ghost guessed:

might be paraphrased as follows: neither the mouth had expressed, nor the mind formed, the thought that the heart had heard of, and the soul surmised. How would you interpret these lines?

P. It could be that the poet wishes to make clear the idea that Margaret had not been told anything about death; she had sensed mortality within herself.

T.   The form of this couplet presents an interesting varia-
     tion on Anglo-Saxon poetry where alliteration appears
     in abundance and the criss-crossing of thought fre-
     quently occurs. Why does it appeal to you?

P.   The clipped effect of the phrases gives the impression
     of precision and conviction. Here is much meaning
     to contemplate in a narrow space.

T.   What is the "blight" man was born for?

P.   The fate of man is mortality. Death is the blight that
     falls not only on the leaves, but on mankind, and of
     course on Margaret as a member of the human race.

> It is the blight man was born for,
> It is Margaret you mourn for.

T.   Why is *blight* an apt word in this context?

P.   The word has a connotation of blemish or disease, but
     it is usually applied to plant life.

T.   John Donne, a seventeenth-century poet and divine,
     in *Meditation XVII* from his *Devotions Upon Emergent
     Occasions,* made the following statements: "The bell
     doth toll for him that thinks it doth .... No man is
     an island, entire of itself; every man is a piece of the
     continent, a part of the main .... And therefore never
     send to know for whom the bell tolls; it tolls for thee."
          It is clear that Donne and Hopkins were both
     reflecting on the fate of man; but with what difference?

P.   John Donne was concerned with the fact that since
     the common fate of man is death, all mankind belongs
     to one great family, and we cannot escape our respon-
     sibility to one another. Hopkins, on the other hand,
     while acknowledging that with every death we suffer
     loss, "It is Margaret you mourn for," is surprised to
     find that an awareness of mortality may arise intuitively

in one so young as Margaret. The last line of the poem sets up a paradox with the opening line, and the questions and contrasts in the first ten lines carry overtones of irony.

T. Why is the title appropriate?

P. It parallels the contrast between youth and age, the child and the adult.

P. Spring and fall are, like life and death, interlocked, interwoven!

P. In the midst of life we are in death.

T. Why is the poem addressed specifically to a *young* child?

P. Without this reference, the full meaning of the poem would be lost.

T. What makes this poem remarkable?

P. It appears to be an original observation on the life of man, expressed in an original form, rhythm, diction, and manner.

P. It is neither a simple statement nor a plain question; it is rather a compact collection of contrasts wrapped in irony and paradox.

P. The climax of the poem

>   Nor mouth had, no nor mind, expressed
>   What heart heard of, ghost guessed:

provides fuel for flights into speculation. It may be that Margaret in her grieving *had not* expressed all the meaning she had felt or experienced; neither had her mind grasped or comprehended all the meaning. Again, it may mean that no mouth or mind *had ever* expressed what she personally had and would experience. And yet again, it may mean that no mouth or mind *can ever* express what she has already felt. Such speculations are extensions rather than contradictions of meaning.

T.   The pursuit of such interpretations is one of the intellectual delights derived from the study of great poetry.

P.   Man's life-long realization of the imminence of death may be the basic theme of the poem. A mood of melancholy broods over it from beginning to end. Its source is the poet's pity for mankind.

P.   The theme may be big and elusive, but the words and images are concrete, precise, and suggestive. The tone is familiar, even pathetically intimate, and the sprung rhythm reinforces this effect.

T.   The poet sees in Margaret the sadness of man caught in this creature predicament called life. Life appears to be little more than the day-to-day experiencing of its own meaning between birth and death. The only thing that seems to have any permanence here is the poet's tender love for Margaret. This is its overtone. Commit this poem to memory: it will sustain your flight through many of life's hurricanes.

A Pattern of Experience

The purpose of questioning is to drill every rift for ore. This means that the driller must know what is ore when he sees it. The ready recognition of good ore depends upon the miner's experience of sampling. To find anything, the searcher must know what he is looking for.

The teacher is out for poetry — not rhymes and rhythms and pleasant pictures, but the poetic interpretation of experience, not philosophical prognostications, but patterns of surmise. He probes and probes until some thought begins to take shape. He estimates its length and depth. The process is slow, but in the long run economical. Eventually new mental experience is uncovered, and we hear and see as Shakespeare so brilliantly exclaimed

The singing masons building roofs of gold.

Such heights can be reached only by a vertical approach, and only in a vertical pattern are the various levels of meaning discernible.

4. *Because I Could Not Stop for Death*

Life, death, and the hereafter have been topics for discussion in all ages and by all kinds of people. Poets and philosophers have never ceased to probe these mysteries for new insights into their meaning. It is not surprising that Emily Dickinson, a young woman of thirty-three living quietly in her father's home at Amherst, Mass. in 1863, should contemplate life, death, and the hereafter. What is surprising, however, is the unique way in which she chooses to speculate on these subjects, and to set down her thoughts about them.

The teacher reads the poem aloud, and then invites the class to read it silently, and to think about it.

Because I Could Not Stop for Death

Because I could not stop for Death,
He kindly stopped for me;
The carriage held but just ourselves
And immortality.

We slowly drove, he knew no haste,
And I had put away
My labour, and my leisure too,
For his civility.

We passed the school where children played
At wrestling in a ring;
We passed the fields of gazing grain,
We passed the setting sun.

> We paused before a house that seemed
> A swelling of the ground;
> The roof was scarcely visible,
> The cornice but a mound.
>
> Since then 'tis centuries; but each
> Feels shorter than the day
> I first surmised the horses' heads
> Were toward eternity.
>
>   — Emily Dickinson

Two or three pupils in turn read the poem aloud.

T.   What is the central image or picture presented? What do you see?

P.   Two people are riding along a country road in a horse-drawn carriage.

T.   Where are they going?

P.   Toward eternity.

T.   Who are these people?

P.   Death and the writer.

T.   Was there anyone else with them?

P.   Yes, <u>Immortality</u>. He may have been the coachman, and perhaps he was driving the horses.

T.   Read the first two stanzas aloud, please.

P.
> Because I could not stop for Death,
> He kindly stopped for me;
> The carriage held but just ourselves
> And Immortality.
>
> We slowly drove, he knew no haste,
> And I had put away
> My labour, and my leisure too,
> For his civility.

T. What is so unusual about the social relationships here described?

P. Death is portrayed as a gallant gentleman who is taking a lady of his choice for a drive.

P. He is probably a prosperous person; he has a carriage, and it is possible that Immortality may be his coachman.

T. Why is this fact left quite indefinite?

P. Life after death is a belief based largely on faith.

T. Has Death any other qualities suggested here?

P. His intentions appear to be amorous.

T. By what words are the symbols of *death* and *love* made interchangeable?

P. "He kindly stopped," "slowly drove," "knew no haste"; he was civil, decent, even genteel.

T. The idea of stopping is used in two different senses in the first two lines. What are they?

P. She was too busy with the daily routines of living to think of death, but Death had time to make a call on her.

T. A paradox is a statement that conflicts with pre-conceived notions. What is paradoxical in these two stanzas?

P. The idea that Death may appear as a courteous and romantic gentleman is somewhat ironical; and, further-more, he is possessed of such charm that he can over-whelm in her mind all thoughts of earthly attachment such as her labour and her leisure.

T. How does form reinforce this intended effect?

P. The rhythms are those of everyday speech, and this effect, along with the near rhymes and clipped lines, creates the impression of something commonplace, or of little significance. The theme, on the other hand, is really very serious and quite profound.

T.   How may the third stanza be a symbolic recapitulation of life?

> We passed the school where children played
> At wrestling in a ring;
> We passed the fields of gazing grain,
> We passed the setting sun.

P.   Children at school or at play are near the beginning of their cycle of existence. The mature grain, ripening in the sun, is waiting for the sickle. The setting sun suggests that the final curtain is about to fall.

T.   In another version of this poem the poet once replaced the second line of this stanza with

> Their lessons scarcely done.

but later she restored the original. Which do you prefer and why? Discussion.

T.   In another version another stanza was added. The suggestion that she is wearing a wedding gown is indicated by "Tippet" and "Tulle." Why do you prefer that this stanza be included or excluded? Discussion.

> We passed the School where Children strove
> At Recess–in the Ring–
> We passed the Fields of Gazing Grain–
> We passed the Setting Sun–
>
> Or rather–He passed Us–
> The Dews drew quivering and chill–
> For only Gossamer, my Gown–
> My Tippet–only Tulle–

At this point discussion may lead to a defence of the third stanza as it appears in the poem. Why provide for these recollections?

P. They are ironically more pleasant than the contemplation of the "sea change" she is experiencing.

T. Please read the fourth stanza aloud, and be ready to explain why its content is so appalling.

P.   We paused before a house that seemed
        A swelling of the ground;
        The roof was scarcely visible,
        The cornice but a mound.

T. What makes all these images so appalling?

P. The reader finds it somewhat shocking to associate with the grave such terms as house, roof, and cornice as applied to "A swelling of the ground."

P. This effect is further emphasized by the brief perfection of the verse and the intensity of the exact imagery. To the poet these things "seemed."

T. Why is "paused" the right verb here?

P. It contrasts aptly with "passed."

P. It suggests a short delay, and not a permanent stop.

P. They may have "paused" briefly at this point for a change of horses.

T. In how many ways does the last stanza differ from the rest of the poem?

        Since then 'tis centuries; but each
        Feels shorter than the day
        I first surmised the horses' heads
        Were toward eternity.

P.   As "we" becomes "I," the whole experience becomes uniquely personal.

P.   There are fewer visual images. The senses are replaced by surmises. Time has become eternity.

P.   Her pretence of familiarity with the posthumous experience of eternity keeps up the paradox, and suggests that the whole of life may be a paradox.

The whole poem is read aloud by several individual pupils.

T.   How does this remarkable poem awaken in us a sense of wonder and awe?

P.   *Immortality* and *eternity* are two of the greatest abstractions known to the mind of man. Both are here presented in distinct and familiar images, with surprising concentration and restraint, but without comment. We are shown what to look at, but not told what to think.

P.   Death, and the disintegration that is supposed to accompany it, are presented as an intensely conscious leave-taking, a romantic undertaking that may be entered into with pleasant anticipation.

T.   The most amazing revelation of this novel and original poem arises from the presentation of a "typical Christian theme in all its final irresolution." The craftsmanship of the poet in achieving so much in so little space makes the poem remarkable.

The *Atlantic Monthly* for March 1957 carried the following tribute to the thought and craft of the great poet. It reads like a comment on the poem under discussion.

To Emily Dickinson

Candid heart,
Too inward to be bold,
Drawn apart
From a thorny world –

Taking leave
Of your twisted lot,
Did you receive
The sacrament you sought?

Did a voice,
Across the darkened air,
Seal the choice
Your vision ventured here,

Or were you still,
As death immured your eyes,
Waiting the call
That countermands surmise?
— John Moffitt

A recapitulation of this discussion reveals seven keys. The establishment of

1. the central image,

2. the irony of the situation,

3. the cycle of human life,

4. the contrast between *passed* and *paused*,

5. the implications of stanza 4,

6. the differences between the last stanza and all the rest,

7. the sources of wonder.

The Complete Poems of Emily Dickinson is now available and "allows the reader to see as a whole the work of an extraordinary poetic genius, the complexity of her personality, the fluctuation of her mood, and the development of her style."

5. *The Shark*

> He seemed to know the harbour,
> So leisurely he swam;
> His fin,
> Like a piece of sheet-iron,
> Three-cornered,
> And with knife-edge,
> Stirred not a bubble
> As it moved
> With its base-line on the water.
>
> His body was tubular
> And tapered,
> And smoke-blue,
> And as he passed the wharf
> He turned,
> And snapped at a flat-fish
> That was dead and floating.
> And I saw the flash of a white throat,
> And a double row of white teeth,
> And eyes of metallic grey,
> Hard and narrow and slit.
>
> Then out of the harbour,
> With that three-cornered fin
> Shearing without a bubble the water
> Lithely,
> Leisurely,
> He swam —
> That strange fish,
> Tubular, tapered, smoke-blue,
> Part vulture, part wolf,
> Part neither — for his blood was cold.
>   — E. J. Pratt.

T. (After silent and oral readings by pupils and teacher.)
Where was the poet probably standing?

P. Perhaps on a wharf.

T. What did he see in the water?

P. A fish.

P. A shark.

P. A sea-monster.

T. Read the first stanza again. What did he actually see?

P. He saw a "fin" cutting through the water.

T. What did it look like?

P. It looked like a piece of sheet-iron, three-cornered, knife-edged, and base-lined.

T. How did it move?

P. Silently, leisurely, even ominously. It seemed unhurried and unchallengeable.

T. Which is the most telling word in the first line? (Discussion).

T. What does "seemed" tell you?

P. Whether or not the shark had been here before, it assumed command. It seemed domineering and imperious.

T. What kind of impression has the poet created?

P. He has given us the impression of something slick, subtle, and sinister.

T. How does the form of the stanza support the meaning and impression?

P. The creature is unusual, and so is the form.

P. The three-cornered words suggest something different from the ordinary.

P. There is no rhyme scheme, and the line-lengths are uneven.

P.   The rhythm, too, is irregular. The accents vary with the positions and meanings of the words.

T.   This is sometimes called the rhythm of meaning rather than the rhythm of form. Matter and method are both unusual, and they enhance each other. Please read aloud the first two stanzas. How is the second stanza connected with the first?

P.   The first deals chiefly with the "fin" and its movement. The second describes the body and the behaviour of the shark.

T.   What did the body look like? (Specific details are collected.) Does the description make the creature appear less or more menacing?

P.   "Shearing" continues the idea of a cutting-edge.

P.   "Smoke-blue," unlike black or white, is an indefinite colour.

P.   A double row of teeth is more menacing and sinister than a single row.

T.   What may be inferred from eyes of "metallic grey"?

P.   The indiscriminate colour of the eyes suggests hardness. The creature is without feeling. The eyes are narrow and cunning, and "slit" suggests slyness and meanness as if the creature were peeping through a mask, and lurking.

T.   How did it turn and why?

P.   To snap up the dead fish off the surface, the scavenger had to turn over on its back, its mouth being on the underside.

T.   How does the form of this stanza enhance its meaning?

P.   It presents again all the irregularities discovered in the first stanza, but in addition by a series of "and's" the poet piles facts upon facts.

T. What does the last stanza add to the previous two? (Please read it aloud.)

P. This stanza describes the shark's withdrawal as the first and the second describe its approach and its passing.

P. This stanza deals specifically with the nature of the creature.

T. What may be inferred from its nature?

P. "Part vulture" suggests that the shark is a scavenger, and "part wolf" that it is a fierce, cruel, predatory creature.

P. It is a cold-blooded killer with vicious, machine-like snapping jaws.

P. It is foreign to the mammal kingdom.

T. What impression did the shark leave behind?

P. That of a creature of strange symmetrical shape and power, endowed with cold ferocity, stealth, cunning, and ruthlessness.

T. Why does the poem awaken a sense of awe and wonder?

P. The shark came from the unknown, and returned again into the unknown.

P. Its mystery was unfathomable and inscrutable, dreadful and deadly.

T. What may have passed through the poet's mind as he watched? A feeling of revulsion, or fascination, or curiosity?

P. Confronted by the inexplicable, he may have wondered why and wherefore such a creature existed, but the shark remained an enigma.

T. A similar problem confronted Blake as he revealed it in his famous poem *The Tiger*.

Who would like to read aloud *The Shark*?

6. *O World*

> O world, thou choosest not the better part!
> It is not wisdom to be only wise,
> And on the inward vision close the eyes,
> But it is wisdom to believe the heart.
> Columbus found a world, and had no chart,
> Save one that faith deciphered in the skies;
> To trust the soul's invincible surmise
> Was all his science and his only art.
> Our knowledge is a torch of smoky pine
> That lights the pathway but one step ahead
> Across a void of mystery and dread.
> Bid, then, the tender light of faith to shine
> By which alone the mortal heart is led
> Unto the thinking of the thought divine.
>
> — George Santayana

T. To whom is the poet speaking?

P. He is addressing the whole world, the general run of mankind.

T. What is he trying to say to us all?

P. We judge too often by appearances.

P. We are inspired by the superficial outward show of things.

T. What, by contrast, should we choose?

P. We should choose to follow the "universal vision" of the heart which feels its way to truth.

T. What other contrasts are apparent in the poem?

P. Knowledge is contrasted, by implication, with wisdom, and intelligence with intuition and instinct.

P. Then, too, sight and insight are contrasted by opposing the light from faith with the light from a smoky torch.

T. In what poetic form has the poet expressed his thought?

P. He has chosen to imitate the sonnet form invented by Petrarch, the Italian poet. The first eight lines (octave) carry the flow of the thought, and the last six (sestet) its ebb.

P. The octave is divided into two clear-cut quatrains, and the sestet into two tercets of sharply defined thoughts.

T. Why is the Petrarchan form appropriate here? How does it enhance the effect of the poem?

P. The theme is exalted. It is a statement followed by a philosophical reflection. The distinct form, like the rhyme scheme, makes the thought compact and helps to clarify its meaning and effect.

T. Briefly, what is the statement made in the first quatrain?

P. The wisdom of the heart (and the spirit) is more reliable than that of the nimble brain.

T. What emotion is the exclamation mark intended to convey?

P. This is his personal conviction, and it is presented as a proclamation.

T. What does the second quatrain add to the first?

P. It serves as an illustration of the thought.

T. Why is Columbus an apt figure in this context?

P. He was an explorer of the unknown. His search was not for gold, but for another way. He surmised that the world was round, and while trying to confirm his belief he came upon America.

P. He set forth into a void without the aid of instruments invented by other men. His faith alone supplied a safer, surer way.

T. What is the relation of the first tercet to the thought expressed in the octave?

P. It is a comment and reflection on it.

T. How does the poet emphasize the helplessness of mankind?

P. A pine torch provides a smoky light. The torch-bearer must progress one step at a time.

P. Finally in the concluding tercet, what does the poet invite (bid) mankind to do?

P. To trim the light of faith in the things of the heart and the spirit.

P. He suggests that even the "mortal" heart can think on things immortal.

The purpose of this brief analysis is to show the inter-relatedness of thought and form. The medium is by no means the message, although it may enhance its effectiveness.

The context of this poem is based on the Christian ethic and the assumption that the soul is immortal. Much of the literature (including Shakespeare) and the history studied in schools likewise presuppose similar beliefs. The humanists, however, regard such cultural concerns as old-fashioned and irrelevant.The form of this poem has been in use for over six hundred years, but zealous hedonists parade their self-centred eroticism in vulgar, formless verse. For both pupils and teachers these facts pose important problems regarding the content and form of contemporary education. How can these questions be resolved, when committees and commissions often merely add to the confusion, and politicians are busy counting votes?

VI

Peaks of Vision

A blast of discordant sounds pounded out of a piano by someone who does not know how to play the instrument may be an expression of freedom and power, but it is not a musical composition. Similarly a plethora of discordant words, no matter how deeply felt, is not a poem. Poetry requires for its existence precision in both conception and execution, but even accurate observation, exact words, and apt images, rhythms, and form are ineffectual unless the poet has control of his feelings and his vision. Without discipline and skill, emotion and vision become wayward and worthless. They are concerned with essences, with particulars and intensities, not spatial magnitudes.

> He who would do good to another must do it in Minute Particulars.
> General Good is the plea of the scoundrel, hypocrite, and flatterer;
> For Art and Science cannot exist but in minutely organized Particulars.
>
> William Blake: *Jerusalem*

Among the many special attributes of imaginative literature is its strange power to regenerate itself in some magical way. Consider the variety of literary masterpieces from the dramas of Shakespeare and the poems of Donne to the plays of Shaw and the novels of Hardy that are still read, studied, or produced today! By means of metaphor, analogy, or parable, imaginative literature has power to extend its own meaning and give off a continuous radiation of meaning to generations of readers. It can invite the reader to come out to meet it, and then confront him with something greater or more important than himself. By means of its verbal delirium it can create a twilight world of wonder, and disclose the unseen and unguessed horizons of the intuitive mind. From things seen and said it can lift the mind's eye to things unseen but meant. Creative literature, furthermore, is latent with a kind of learning that cannot be found elsewhere. Any system of education that is so concerned with its pragmatic social pursuits that it cannot accommodate the intangibles is devoid of vision!

1. *Wonder Is Not Precisely Knowing*

As a poet Emily Dickinson (1830-86) was unique. Between 1852, the date of the publication of her first poem, and her death, she composed 1775 short poems, only three or four of which were ever published in her lifetime. At first she sought advice and longed for encouragement, but no one appeared wise enough to guide her. This, perhaps, was a blessing because it forced her back upon her genius, and left her free to follow the unfettered way of her spontaneous spirit. Although every poem in both matter and method is remarkable, the following one presents a good example of the spare and sinewy expression of her genius working at the peak of vision. Her definition of wonder is much more finely honed than that given in any dictionary.

Wonder Is Not Precisely Knowing

Wonder is not precisely knowing,
And not precisely knowing not;
A beautiful but bleak condition
He has not lived who has not felt.

Suspense is his maturer sister;
Whether adult delight is pain
Or of itself a new misgiving—
This is the gnat that mangles men.

Wonder is neither precisely to know nor precisely not to know, i.e. it has little to do with knowing. It occurs somewhere between the known and the unknown. Its nature is equivocal, beautiful but bleak. He who has not felt this condition has either not lived at all or not known what it is to live in earnest. In stanza two "his" may refer to wonder or to a presupposed wonderer. Suspense is either a painful delight or a new doubt leading to further wonder. "Gnat" refers to both the sting of the insect and the battering ram of the Great Negation. The ambiguity of "wonder" is ambiguously stated.

Emily Dickinson often used some images and violent contrasts, such as "gnat that mangles" to shock the reader into awareness. Near-rhymes and metrical inversions often disrupt formal patterns to reflect the unexpectedness of the thought. Intensity and spontaneity of feeling, clear, cool precision in the choice of words, and whimsical rhythms characterize her short cryptic poems. It is the originality and freshness of the visions, however, that astonish and intrigue the reader.

Obliged by circumstance to live most of her life in seclusion and attendance upon ailing parents, she found some solace in composing poems for her sister Lavinia's children and their friends. Without the transitory adulations of the world, her creative spirit thrived in the pursuit of her own instincts and insights. She called herself "a private poet." Genius was her spur. At the centre of her nature was a feeling of surmise that set her visions vibrating with integrity. She harboured what someone has described as "spiritual conviction without commitment to belief." When she died, she left hundreds of her poems stuffed away in cupboards and closets of the spacious family home at Amherst, Massachusetts. Her gift to American literature, and to the art of poetry in particular, was unique!

2. *A Noiseless, Patient Spider*

Some of the greatest thoughts that man has contemplated have been clarified and made communicable by means of contrasts, comparisons, or analogies. It has been said that we think in contrasts. Walt Whitman used an analogy between a spider and his own soul to point up his own spiritual groping.

A Noiseless, Patient Spider

A noiseless, patient spider,
I mark'd, where, on a little promontory, it stood, isolated;
Mark'd how, to explore the vacant, vast surrounding,
It launched forth filament, filament, filament, out of itself;
Ever unreeling them, ever tirelessly speeding them.

And you, O my Soul, where you stand,
Surrounded, detached, in measureless oceans of space,
Ceaselessly musing, venturing, throwing–seeking the
    spheres, to connect them;
Till the bridge you will need, be form'd, till the ductile
    anchor hold;
Till the gossamer thread you fling, catch somewhere, O my
    Soul.

In order to appreciate fully the force and aptness of Whitman's analogy, it is necessary to know something about the habits of some spiders.

On sunny autumn days when young spiders break from their cocoons, they climb up tall blades of grass or some similar object and begin to send forth out of their tiny bodies slender strands of silk to float freely in the air. Air currents extend these filaments still further until they have enough buoyancy to lift the little spider into the air. On quiet autumn mornings millions of these tiny threads may be seen against the sun wafting their ancient microscopic balloonists into the upper air and away to distant parts. Spiders are the most abundant of creatures found in the upper air, and some have been discovered at fifteen thousand feet above the earth swinging along like happy aerialists on strands of shimmering silk.

This natural phenomenon must have been familiar to Walt Whitman, because he describes the spider's habits in the first stanza of this poem with great precision. As a consequence he beholds his Soul as an aerialist suspended between earth and heaven in measureless oceans of space, seeking to connect the two spheres, hoping to find an anchorage to "catch somewhere" in another world of experience. Without the analogy with the spider, Whitman's poor soul's "musing, venturing, throwing" would have little meaning.

3. *Nightingales*

Beautiful must be the mountains whence ye come,
And bright in the fruitful valleys the streams, wherefrom
Ye learn your song:
Where are those starry woods? O might I wander there,
Among the flowers, which in that heavenly air
Bloom the year long?

Nay, barren are those mountains and spent the streams:
Our song is the voice of desire, that haunts our dreams,
    A throe of the heart,
Whose pining visions dim, forbidden hopes profound,
  No dying cadence nor long sigh can sound,
    For all our art.

Alone, aloud in the raptured ear of men
We pour our dark nocturnal secret; and then,
    As night is withdrawn
From these sweet-springing meads and bursting boughs of May,
  Dream, while the innumerable choir of day
    Welcome the dawn.

                              – Robert Bridges

Nightingales are night-singing birds whose songs have for
centuries won praise in many parts of Europe and Asia.
Although nightingales are neither seen nor heard in
Canada, this need not be an obstacle to interpretation.
It should engage the imagination more deeply and
heighten the mystery surrounding the source of the nightingales' beautiful songs. Although beauty is the theme of
the poem, the nightingales' explanation of the origin
haunts the mind.

    In the first stanza the poet suggests that the birds must
dwell in some romantically beautiful mountain fastness
where they learn their songs from the streams that run
through fertile valleys, and where peace, beauty, light, and
sound are everlasting and do not fluctuate with the seasons.
He does not know where those starlit woods may be, but
he yearns to breathe their paradisaic air. The antiphonal
effect of the short line sounds like an echo, and reminds
one of a chant. The rhythm and lilt of the poem may
reflect the beauty of the nightingales' songs.

    In the remainder of the poem the birds reject the poet's
suggestion. Their songs come not from barren mountains

or streams whose melodies are spent, but from the heart, from desire rising in the heart like a throb, a pang, a spasm, an agony, or a convulsion such as may be experienced when something is created and brought forth new into the world. In spite of their condition as creatures of this earth their desires and hopes are for perfection. In spite of their yearning for clearer visions, plaintive melodies, and artistic craft they cannot plumb the depths or heights of beauty. Alone with their intrinsic power and under the cover of darkness they pour their troubled melody into the spellbound ears of men. Before dawn they withdraw to dream again of beauty and leave the blossoming meadows to all the other creatures, men included. The natural beauty from which the poet thought the nightingales had drawn their inspiration was left behind for others to enjoy, albeit ineffectually.

From the poem certain important thoughts concerning art and inspiration may be inferred. Like the nightingales, the poet, or any other artist for that matter, cannot take the full measure of beauty. Inspiration is not a product of group dynamics, panel discussions, political conventions, educational conferences, or religious conclaves. It is experienced by individuals "alone," i.e. in solitude, and a special or beautiful setting is unnecessary for its inception. Another inference may be that as nightingales are compared to other birds, so artists may be related to the rest of mankind. The songs of the nightingales and the poets may make man more sensitive and responsive to beauty. Where and how the artist lives have nothing to do with the case.

It appears to be the fate of man to dream of a perfection beyond his ability to grasp or apprehend because it is forbidden by his creatureship. Man, nevertheless, desires, hopes, and strives. As Emily Dickinson wrote

This is the gnat that mangles men.

As we study a literary masterpiece we soon become aware
of an ineffable quality, a meaning implied in the work
of art that overflows our attempts to interpret and the
power of words to express. Our temptation then is to cir-
cumscribe the unknown and reduce it to the dimensions
of the known, i.e. to the terms of our conventional, concep-
tual knowledge. Our aim is not to experience beauty or
wonder and thus to apprehend a more abundant life, but
rather to comprehend, evaluate, and explain the tangible
and the trite. A great poem then becomes a pale reflection
of the reality that transcends it. All art refuses to be
"managed." Whence comes poetic insight and inspiration?
Somewhere in the intuitive imagination shines the spark
that ignites the image at a poem's centre. Just so, the artist
might reply, but the nightingales would answer from "the
voice of desire."

A few years ago a visiting lecturer, imported at considerable expense, to explain the delights of poetry,
read *Nightingales* aloud and then dismissed it as a collection
of fanciful images and winsome sounds, a beautiful lyric,
sad but lovely. The gentle lady confessed to a passionate
love of poetry, but she had failed completely to apprehend
what Robert Bridges was trying to say.

If the sensitive people of the next generation are to
see visions and dream dreams they had better be taught
today to read precisely what the best experiencers of the
past have left behind in their writings.

4. *Before the World Was Made*

> If I make the lashes dark
> And the eyes more bright
> And the lips more scarlet,
> Or ask if all be right
> From mirror after mirror,
> No vanity's displayed:
> I'm looking for the face I had
> Before the world was made.

What if I look upon a man
As though on my beloved,
And my blood be cold the while
And my heart unmoved?
Why should he think me cruel
Or that he is betrayed?
I'd have him love the thing that was
Before the world was made.
       — William Butler Yeats

In this charming little lyric a profound insight into a common human predicament is delivered with a gentle impact upon the spirit. The history of the painted face is long and variegated. The young lady here presented, denies that her use of cosmetics is an expression of vanity. In spite of her pathetic weariness of effort she persists in her search for the ideal natural beauty to which she feels that she was originally entitled. She may not succeed by artificial means, but her mention of a mask is better than no attempt at all to reclaim her lost birthright.

In the second stanza she seeks the ideal of genuine love by pretending to act the part of a lover. Her painted mask and false personality are not intended to deceive or betray anyone. Her ideal of both beauty and love may have been lost in her evolution through a cold, drab, polluted world, but by artful means she hopes to reclaim, at least in part, her primordial ideals.

How many millions of people have lived their lives in search of the ideals that they felt, had circumstance not intervened, rightfully belonged to them? How dull life would be, did not such hopes exist!

5. *The Tuft of Flowers*

Occasionally it is profitable to observe the results of creative reading in reverse. Suppose that we entertained the following beliefs:

1. That this world is contracting rapidly into a single, socialized whole;
2. That men and nations are becoming closely integrated and interdependent;
3. That the past and the future are bound together in the present:
4. That the same flash of beauty or truth or goodness that surprised a beholder ten thousand years ago and caused him to catch his breath in wonder may today give anyone of us reason to pause and reflect;
5. That a plain and simple experience may secrete its own particular insight;
6. That we are responsible for preserving for posterity the fragments of wisdom transmitted to us!

Suppose that we harboured such beliefs and wished to communicate them to others in a memorable form. How would we set about the task? Fifty years ago Robert Frost solved the problem for himself this way:

The Tuft of Flowers

I went to turn the grass once after one
Who mowed it in the dew before the sun.

The dew was gone that made his blade so keen
Before I came to view the leveled scene.

I looked for him behind an isle of trees;
I listened for his whetstone on the breeze.

But he had gone his way, the grass all mown,
And I must be, as he had been, − alone,

'As all must be,' I said within my heart,
'Whether they work together or apart.'

But as I said it, swift there passed me by
On noiseless wing a bewildered butterfly,

Seeking with memories grown dim o'er night
Some resting flower of yesterday's delight.

And once I marked his flight go round and round
As where some flower lay withering on the ground.

And then he flew as far as eye could see,
And then on tremulous wing came back to me.

I thought of questions that have no reply,
And would have turned to toss the grass to dry;

But he turned first, and led my eye to look
At a tall tuft of flowers beside a brook,

A leaping tongue of bloom the scythe had spared
Beside a reedy brook the scythe had bared.

The mower in the dew had loved them thus,
By leaving them to flourish, not for us,

Nor yet to draw one thought of ours to him,
But from sheer morning gladness at the brim.

The butterfly and I had lit upon,
Nevertheless, a message from the dawn,

That made me hear the wakening birds around,
And hear his long scythe whispering to the ground,

And feel a spirit kindred to my own;
So that henceforth I worked no more alone;

But glad with him, I worked as with his aid,
And weary, sought at noon with him the shade;

And dreaming, as it were, held brotherly speech
With one whose thought I had not hoped to reach.

'Men work together,' I told him from the heart,
'Whether they work together or apart.'

–Robert Frost

Glancing back at the assumptions made concerning the ideas and suggestions latent in the poem, we find that these prosaic opinions do not challenge the mind with the possibility of new horizons. The essence of the poetry, on the other hand, is found in the poet's delight in feeling "sheer morning gladness at the brim" and in hearing in imagination another's "long scythe whispering to the ground" as "a leaping tongue of bloom" is spared to express "a message from the dawn" of both time and eternity. In imagination the poet holds "brotherly speech" with a "spirit kindred," and so may we. And in the classroom study of the poem, the excitement of discovery creates its own discipline.

Should anyone still be unconvinced of the power concealed in great literature to stir the intellect, excite the imagination, or stimulate the curiosity, let him contemplate Robert Frost's most pungent couplet:

Forgive, O Lord, my little jokes on Thee
And I'll forgive Thy great big one on me.

Or this, his most famous couplet,

We dance round in a ring and suppose
But the Secret sits in the middle and knows.

Or the profundity of this one,

Security makes men weak
Freedom makes men meek.

Or the power of Robert Frost's genius in the use of words to create wonder in the mind of the reader.

Questioning Faces

> The winter owl banked just in time to pass
> And save herself from breaking window glass,
> And her wings straining suddenly aspread
> Caught color from the last of evening red
> In a display of underdown and quill
> To glassed-in children at the window sill.

Wordsworth would have described this as "authentic tidings of invisible things," and Frost himself said "A poem begins in delight and ends in wisdom."

The teaching of a great poem resembles in some respects a heart-transplant operation. Sloughing off massive technical details, the teacher plucks the heart out of the poet's mystery and transfers it to the heart of the pupil's mystery. There, if not rejected, it may bring about a marriage of minds. Perhaps the greatest benevolence literature can bestow is the variety of insights it provides into other people's minds.

Since the main concern of the teacher of literature is not appreciation but nourishment, you may ask, what are some of the signs of the pupil's maturing?

1. His inclination to look at life, his own and that of others, as an artistic whole with all parts integrated in a vertical pattern.
2. Ability to make choices, to distinguish between what is essential and what is irrelevant in television, radio, sports, and reading; to grasp ideas quickly, provoke questions, resolve doubts, reason logically, and adjust readily to changing images, rhythms, and patterns of feeling; to excite his own self-starter before it is rusted solid.

3. Recognition that personal resources alone are inadequate or insufficient for the solution of many problems, that self-criticism, control, and poise are greatly enhanced by observing the experience of others in literature.

4. Realization that every individual, nevertheless, has secrets that lie outside the group and cannot be included in the group. Everyone is an island in the archipelago of co-operation and compromise, but he should refuse to be typed, classified, standardized, and rendered functional. Literature may help to keep him free.

5. Readiness to act with decision to stand up to the crowded conditions of life and work in today's world, without losing the quietness and strength of his own inner life at the centre. The cultivation of an attitude of life that is strengthened, rather than defeated, by the experiences of living, real or vicarious, as observed in literature.

6. A capacity to be moved, even inspired, by acts of kindness, sacrifice, and goodness as revealed in life and in literature.

7. A personal vision of life as a work of art with a point of view that is poised and insighted because the artist serves a vision of possibilities.

To anyone who asks, Has the study of literature any practical purpose? we reply that these are a few of the values that may be derived from the reading of inspiring masterpieces. The literature of creative reading can help us all to advance to the frontiers of wisdom where we may stand breathless in a wild surmise:

Silent, upon a peak in Darien.

6. *Dover Beach*

> The sea is calm to-night.
> The tide is full, the moon lies fair
> Upon the straits, on the French coast the light
> Gleams and is gone; the cliffs of England stand,
> Glimmering and vast, out in the tranquil bay.
> Come to the window, sweet is the night-air!
> Only, from the long line of spray
> Where the sea meets the moon-blanch'd land,
> Listen! you hear the grating roar
> Of pebbles which the waves draw back and fling,
> At their return, up the high strand,
> Begin, and cease, and then again begin,
> With tremulous cadence slow, and bring
> The eternal note of sadness in.
>
> Sophocles long ago
> Heard it in the Aegean, and it brought
> Into his mind the turbid ebb and flow
> Of human misery; we
> Find also in the sound a thought,
> Hearing it by this distant northern sea.
>
> The Sea of Faith
> Was once, too, at the full, and round earth's shore
> Lay like the folds of a bright girdle furl'd,
> But now I only hear
> Its melancholy, long, withdrawing roar,
> Retreating, to the breath
> Of the night-wind, down the vast edges drear
> And naked shingles of the world.
>
> Ah, love, let us be true
> To one another! for the world, which seems
> To lie before us like a land of dreams,
> So various, so beautiful, so new,
> Hath really neither joy, nor love, nor light,

> Nor certitude, nor peace, nor help for pain;
> And we are here as on a darkling plain
> Swept with a confused alarms of struggle and flight,
> Where ignorant armies clash by night,
>   — Mathew Arnold

Was Arnold lamenting the decline of religious faith or pleading for a renewal of personal love as man's only salvation in a confused and troubled world?

> Ah, love, let us be true
> To one another!

Although this is a personal appeal to someone near and dear, it has a wider application. The poet invites us all to come to the window and to look and listen as he interprets the signs of the times. His passionate desire is to share his experiences with others. The peace of the night is vast and deep. It is the surging surf that brings "the eternal note of sadness in." Sophocles heard that same sound twenty-three hundred years ago. He, too, heard in the roar of the sea the universal cry of human misery. Arnold, on the other hand, harboured in his heart the thought that much of the disorder and confusion in the world flowed from a decline of faith. A belief in the infinite values of life that had once bound together the peoples of the world was ebbing and retreating and presumably not coming back. It was a melancholy thought as he contrasted the bright with the drear and appearances with reality, and envisaged a world empty of feeling and meaning. Personal love was the only certainty left! The irregularity of the line-length, metre, and rhyme scheme enhanced the effect of the poet's agonizing over the human misery that he perceived in the world. The poem is neither a religious lament nor a love lyric. It is an ardent, eloquent, and dramatic appeal for a return to basic values.

VII

Shakespeare's Art and Craft

1. *The Fringe Benefits of Shakespeare's Mind*

Titles are often invented to awaken curiosity. This one is not, although it may mislead. It is rather an attempt to gather together several ideas into a knot of words that expresses a single thought. Some of the threads in this ball of yarn might be called Shakespeare's Intuitive Declarations, or Intuitive Confidences, or Intuitive Intimations, or Shakespeare as Artist of Intuitions. Common to all the threads is the idea that intuition rather than intellect was the original stuff from which Shakespeare's massive tapestries were woven. Or to put it another way, it may be conceded by some that the intellect is at its best when intuitive. The formal, operational, analytical machine-work of the reason is everywhere apparent in a work of art, but the artist behind the design relied all the while, as confidently as a mystic, on his native instinct, insight, and intuition – on the bits of fluff that were wafted in over the fringe of his mind.

> We are such stuff
> As dreams are made on; and our little life
> Is rounded with a sleep.
> *The Tempest*

113

This complex combination of simple words, rhythmic and impressive and totally devoid of literary affectation or ornament, is as fragile as thistledown and as unscientific as faith. It expresses a poetic truth that dances over the airy threshold of the mind, at once strange and familiar. Shakespeare has said so many things superlatively well that the fringe benefits of his mind have become memorable.

> There's a divinity that shapes our minds
> Rough-hew them how we will . . . .
> > *Hamlet*

> There is some soul of goodness in things evil,
> Would men observingly distil it out . . . .
> > *Henry V*

> It is a heretic that makes the fire
> Not she which burns in't . . . .
> > *The Winter's Tale*

> The lunatic, the lover, and the poet
> Are of imagination all compact . . . .
> > *A Midsummer Night's Dream*

> But look, the morn, in russet mantle clad
> Walks o'er the dew of yon high eastward hill . . . .
> > *Hamlet*

Some of Shakespeare's casual observations have become proverbial sayings:

"The better part of valour is discretion."

"Thus conscience doth make cowards of us all."

"The course of true love never did run smooth."

"Though this be madness, yet there is method in it."

"Assume a virtue if you have it not."

"Brevity is the soul of wit."

The figurative picturesqueness of Shakespeare's language gathered to itself startling patterns on the fringe of his mind where fact and fancy commingled with abandon, and many of these phrases are common coin today:

> "A King of shreds and patches."
>
> "More in sorrow than in anger."
>
> "A man more sinned against than sinning."
>
> "Cudgel thy brains."
>
> "Pluck the heart out of my mystery."
>
> "I know a trick worth two of that."

J. W. MacKail has warned us: "It is essential not to treat any single figure in the plays, or any single thing said, as isolated." Students of Shakespeare, of course, will have no difficulty in recalling the contexts of these observations that apply to situations today with surprising aptness.

> A snapper-up of unconsidered trifles ....
> *The Winter's Tale*

> The nature of bad news infects the teller ....
> *Anthony and Cleopatra*

> The web of our life is of a mingled yarn, good and ill together, our virtues would be proud if our faults whipped them not; and our crimes would despair if they were not cherished by our own virtues.
> *All's Well That Ends Well*

> Study is like the heaven's glorious sun,
> That will not be deep search'd with saucy looks;
> Small have continual plodders ever won,
> Save base authority from others' books.....
> *Love's Labour's Lost*

> At Christmas I no more desire a rose
> Than wish a snow in May's new-fangled mirth;
> But like of each thing that in season grows.....
> *Love's Labour's Lost*

No other writer developed the full richness of the English language as did Shakespeare. No other writer can match his multiform use of the same word; the gradations of distinctive impressions conveyed; his coined words, pregnant with significance, suited to his purpose and precisely fitted to his ideas; his choice of appropriate, accurate, and forceful epithets; his conciseness when necessary, and the luxuriant flow of words at other times.

Shakespeare's implications become our inferences, and were it not that we, too, are intuitive, sensitive, and imaginatively alert we should not be able to understand him at all. The best of Shakespeare is found in the intended meanings with which his words are laden, be they flashes of verbal inspiration such as *cold comfort, trumpet-tongued, cloud-capped, honey-heavy, helter-skelter, hugger-mugger, skimble-skamble,* or interpretations of man's earthly predicament in whole plays such as a man's loneliness of spirit in *Hamlet* or a man's spiritual adventures at playing God in *King Lear.*

Over the fringe of Shakespeare's receptive mind came an incalculable variety of seed-grain, the chaff blown away, to germinate on contact and sprout in such profusion that his intellect was at its wit's end to keep an orderly pattern in the seed-bed. Other dramatists, including some of his contemporaries, could draw more clearly defined plots and characters, but no one, before or since, has been blessed with so fertile a creative mind as Shakespeare possessed. The soil of his mind was rich and friable, the light of his spirit shone brightly upon it, and the warmth of his emotions was all-pervading.

A change of comparison may help to clarify the meaning further. All was honey that came to his hive, but his adventurous bees went foraging for quality. Within the focus of the mind lay fields of clover, flecked with daisies; on and beyond the fringe of his mental landscape, however, grew rosemary and rue, mints and marigolds, rose-buds and bergamot, and

> . . .daffodils
> That come before the swallow dares, and take
> The winds of March with beauty.
>
> *The Winter's Tale*

The flavour of the honey from Shakespeare's happy hive
was, as noted even in his lifetime, richer than that of his
contemporaries'.

William Kempe, Robert Gough, Richard Robinson are
all listed among the players in the First Folio, and all are
also named among the Cambridge Graduates of 1584-
1592. For those whom the learned professions of the
day could not claim, the stage held attractions and provided
outlets for creative energy. Some graduates sought prefer-
ment as playwrights, but they lasted only for a day. Robert
Greene, M.A., 1583, made his exit in 1592 on a combination
of pickled herring and Rhenish wine. Thomas Nash, B.A.,
1586, took leave of this world in 1601 after a sojourn in
Fleet Street prison. Kit Marlowe, M.A., 1587, was done in
by Francis Archer in a tavern brawl in 1593. Had the
Canada Council then existed, one wonders which one of
these wits would have been eligible for a grant of financial
aid. Would Shakespeare have qualified?

While the university wits were striving to secure a brief
place in the sun, Shakespeare, with the sporadic encouragement of his patron, Southampton, M.A., 1589, was making steady progress with one popular success after another
and was leading "the questing mind to pioneer among
adventures that are strange and new." No one then knew,
nor could foresee the genius that was "made of sterner
stuff," that in his "coign of vantage" had found "metal
more attractive," and by force of "yeoman service" was making "a palpable hit." A magical facility and felicity of expression in which word and thought fitted each other were
habitual with him. His graphic directness, luminous sim-
plicity of phrase, and imaginative splendour of diction

awakened an echo of instinctive recognition in all who
came for entertainment to the *Globe Theatre*, his "Wooden
O." Contemporary playwrights sought dramatic effects by
means of suggestion, extravagance, and surprise. Their
characters are theatrical figures, demonstrable spectacles.
Shakespeare's characters are true to life. They share their
humanity with us.

While university authorities at Oxford and Cambridge
were anxious, even to the extent of using bribes, to keep
professional players off their precincts, the Corporation
of Oxford town entertained touring companies such as
that to which Shakespeare belonged. It is altogether likely
that Shakespeare enacted the part of the Ghost when
Hamlet was presented there to the townsfolk. Shakespeare
passed through Oxford many times on his journeyings
between London and Stratford, and tradition makes him
an intimate of the family of John Davenant, the landlord
of the Crown Inn at Oxford. John Davies, a calligrapher
settled at Oxford, paid warm tributes to Shakespeare in
his lifetime for the "quality" of his compositions. William
Goodyeare, himself an author of some repute, was the
landlord of *The Mermaid* in London when Shakespeare
first came there, and he in turn was probably kinsman
to Sir Henry Goodyeare who adopted Michael Drayton
"Since there's no help, come let us kiss and part" as a
small child. The theatre, taverns, and thoroughfares in
and about London formed the corridors of Shakespeare's
university. How well he learned his lessons may be judged
on the verdict of his achievement. His plays are still enjoyed
by the majority and approved by the minority. He recon-
ciled the precious with the popular. The enchantment of
The Tempest may have had its foundation in Shakespeare's
transmutation of the realistic descriptions provided by a
half-inebriated sailor who in 1609 had been cast ashore
on the island of Bermuda with Sir George Somers. One
wonders if Shakespeare bought him another drink. What

Shakespeare did for Holinshed and for Plutarch is enough to convince one of the transmigration of souls. He created his own world of very lusty people. To contemplate what the universities could have done for him is a waste of good speculative time. Without them, he knew instinctively that King Arthur and the Round Table were not for him.

Tradition claims that Shakespeare was "very good company" and yet "not a company-keeper." Like so many men of genius he probably lived a lonely life, forever looking for excuses to be away with his thoughts. Like Hamlet he may have been preoccupied with his own plans, his own visions, his own ends. It is not unlikely that this man of "quality," trading his talents unobtrusively in the intellectual market-place of his day, quite unaware that one day he would be called "the master workman," "the great architect in the guild of letters," "the prophet of the human soul," hoped most to get away from it all, to return to Stratford, to buy the best house in the town, and to settle down as a substantial and respected burgher. His dream come true, he might well have withdrawn from London with Antony's words upon his lips as the Roman mob began to jostle him:

> Nay, press not so upon me, stand far off.

All this may help to illustrate how little, after nearly four hundred years, we know about the man whose fame has spread throughout the world, whose masterpieces of creative art have drawn the homage of the intellectual fraternity of mankind, whose dramas, along with the King James version of the Bible, have done more to advance the cause of peace among men than any rocket attack upon Mars itself can ever do.

Why does Shakespeare in his achievements stand apart, detached yet not aloof, ubiquitous yet still unique? What is the difference between the mind of Shakespeare and that of Ben Jonson, or Francis Bacon, or Bernard Shaw? The difference lies in Shakespeare's strong intuitive sense and imaginative *insight*, in the merry dance of ideas that frolicked on the fringe of his resilient mind, in his ability to play the theme and the variations on the theme at one and the same time. "In Shakespeare's own phrase," says Moulton, "we have 'the law of writ and the liberty': rules of art vanish in the higher law of inspired creative liberty." Believing this, we may be no nearer to plucking the heart out of the mystery that is Othello, or Falstaff, or Feste, or Rosalind, or Richard, or Caliban, or Ariel, but we may be better able to appreciate the magic of Shakespeare's creative power. To a prosaic mind *Macbeth* is a story about ambition, recited in the horizontal sequence of *and then, and then, and then* of detective fiction; to a poetic mind it may be a study in demonology built in vertical pattern, a whole composed of many parts and facets. Surely no one would presume to say that Shakespeare meant only this and nothing else! Shakespeare's hints and hunches ring true today because in his own time they rang true. Man's mind and spirit appeared to be his hunting ground.

"In most plays," writes Clutton-Brock, "we watch to see what will happen next, but at the height of *Hamlet* and *King Lear* this anxiety about the course of events ceases; the dramatic action seems to fade away and the material conflict to be stilled, so that we may see souls independent of time and place. Hamlet and Lear are terribly beset by circumstances; but, when they are most beset, they escape into a solitude of their own minds where we are alone with them and overhear their innermost secrets. Then the dramatic action seems to have had no object except to lead them into this solitude, where speech becomes thought, and there are no longer any events except those of the soul."–(A. Clutton-Brock: *The Unworldliness of Shakespeare*)

At this point one may wonder how Shakespeare composed his plays. Did he begin with the opening line

If music be the food of love, play on,

and work through scenes sequential to the end, producing something like the First Folio or a modern editor's text? Or did he begin with episodes, much as a harassed director (or stage manager in his day) would do, and work the parts, backward and forward, with dramatic revisions and fresh insights into a whole that would best express his whole meaning. It is more than likely that the second method was his way of work. The plays are not primarily narratives, but revelations, not poetic dramas but dramatic poems, equally rewarding on the stage or in the study. "I cannot help being of the opinion," wrote Charles Lamb, "that the plays of Shakespeare are less calculated for performance on a stage than those of almost any other dramatist whatever. Their distinguishing excellence is a reason that they should be so. There is so much in them which comes not under the province of acting, with which eye and tone and gesture have nothing to do."

Three Stratfords are now busy with theatrical interpretations of the famous plays. It is, nevertheless, in the classrooms, the libraries, and the armchairs of the world that Shakespeare's mind finds the mirror for its flame. There, time provides the respite for reflection. There, the reader's intuition grows by what it feeds on. Those who know the plays best by study, enjoy them most upon the stage. Perhaps no one has ever understood the theatre better than Shakespeare, but no one surely would concede that his spirit was ever confined to such a cage. In full flight his imagination sings upon the wing in the rhapsody of its own well-being, as follows:

> True: therefore doth heaven divide
> The state of man in divers functions,
> Setting endeavour in continual motion;
> To which is fixed, as an aim or butt,
> Obedience: for so work the honey-bees,
> Creatures that by a rule in nature teach
> The act of order to a peopled kingdom.
> They have a king and officers of sorts;
> Where some, like magistrates, correct at home,
> Others, like merchants, venture trade abroad,
> Others, like soldiers, armed in their stings,
> Make boot upon the summer's velvet buds,
> Which pillage they with merry march bring home
> To the tent-royal of their emperor;
> Who, busied in his majesty, surveys
> The singing masons building roofs of gold,
> The civil citizens kneading up the honey,
> The poor mechanic porters crowding in
> Their heavy burdens at his narrow gate,
> The sad-eyed justice, with his surly hum,
> Delivering o'er to executors pale
> The lazy yawning drone.
>
> *Henry V*

Such a rhapsodical passage may benefit from the oral delivery of a good actor, but what can an actor add to a passage like the following:

> Merciful Heaven!
> Thou rather with thy sharp and sulphurous bolt
> Split'st the unwedgeable and gnarled oak
> Than the soft myrtle; but man, proud man,
> Drest in a little brief authority,
> Most ignorant of what he's most assur'd,
> His glassy essence, like an angry ape,
> Plays such fantastic tricks before high heaven,
> As make the angels weep; who with our spleens,
> Would all themselves laugh mortal.
>
> *Measure for Measure*

The speech is over before one has decided whether "Merciful Heaven!" is an exclamation or an apostrophe. The passage itself is well worth careful study for the insights that the poet's mind could accommodate at one and the same time.

The songs of dainty Ariel, on the other hand, the loveliest in all Shakespeare,

> Come unto these yellow sands

> Full fathom five thy father lies

or

> Where the bee sucks, there suck I
> In a cowslip's bell I lie;
> There I couch when owls do cry.
> On the bat's back I do fly
> After summer merrily;
> Merrily, merrily shall I live now
> Under the blossom that hangs on the bough.

These songs need the voice and musical accompaniment to palpitate the heart of their mystery. Not so Lear's pathetic and profound call to Cordelia:

> Come, let's away to prison;
> We two alone will sing like birds i' the cage:
> When thou dost ask me blessing, I'll kneel down,
> And ask of thee forgiveness: so we'll live,
> And pray, and sing, and tell old tales, and laugh
> At gilded butterflies, and hear poor rogues
> Talk of court news; and we'll talk with them too,
> Who loses and who wins; who's in, who's out;
> And take upon's the mystery of things
> As if we were God's spies: and we'll wear out,
> In a wall'd prison, packs and sets of great ones
> That ebb and flow by the moon.
> > *King Lear*

In such a passage the dawn of the spirit breaks across "the insubstantial pageant" of the theatre, the Stratfords become theatrical and trite, and the drama takes place in the eye of Shakespeare's vision and on the fringe of our pursuing minds.

Shakespeare's genius stands apart because his free-flying creative spirit refused to be "cabin'd, cribb'd, confin'd" by rules of literary writ. Nowhere is this more apparent than in his creation of a Fools' Paradise in which not all the folly or the foolery is confined to clowns and jesters. Wit, humour, and irony abound throughout the plays. The poet's genius is fancy free, fresh, vigorous, and daring.

Lepidus: What manner o' thing is your crocodile?
Antony: It is shaped, sir, like itself, and it is as broad as it hath breadth; it is just so high as it is, and moves with its own organs; it lives by that which nourisheth it; and the elements once out of it, it transmigrates.
Lepidus: What colour is it of?
Antony: Of its own colour too.
Lepidus: 'Tis a strange serpent.
Antony: 'Tis so! and the tears of it are wet.

Antony and Cleopatra

Hamlet: Do you see yonder cloud that's almost in shape of a camel?
Polonius: By the mass, and 'tis like a camel, indeed.
Hamlet: Methinks it is like a weasel.
Polonius: It is backed like a weasel.
Hamlet: Or like a whale?
Polonius: Very like a whale.

Hamlet

Falstaff confesses his own sins and laughs at his own follies, and we love him for it. "Dost thou hear, Hal? thou knowest in the state of innocency Adam fell; and what should poor Jack Falstaff do in the days of villany? Thou seest I have

more flesh than another man; and therefore more frailty."
(*Henry IV, Pt. I*)

Falstaff leads us into a world of infinite freedom where
moral and civil laws appear absurd and where "to banish
plump Jack" is to "banish all the world."

"A goodly portly man, i' faith, and a corpulent; of a
cheerful look, a pleasing eye, and a most noble carriage
... and now I remember me, his name is Falstaff: if that
man should be lewdly given, he deceiveth me; for Harry,
I see virtue in his looke."

Thus disarmed we are delighted when he says "What
need I be so forward with him that calls not on me? Well,
'tis no matter; honour pricks me on. Yes, but how if honour
prick me off when I come on? How then? Can honour
set to a leg? No. Or an arm? No. Or take away the grief
of a wound? No. Honour hath no skill in surgery then?
No. What is honour? A word. What is that word honour?
Air. A trim reckoning! Who hath it? He that died o'
Wednesday. Doth he feel it? No. Doth he hear it? No.
It is insensible then? Yea, to the dead. But will it not live
with the living? No. Why? Detraction will not suffer it.
Therefore I'll none of it: honour is a mere scutcheon:
and so ends my cathechism." (*Henry IV, Pt. I*)

Who but Shakespeare would dare to introduce a long
temperance lecture into Act I, Sc. IV, of *Hamlet,* just before
the entrance of the Ghost? Who but Shakespeare could
hold attention, especially at midnight when the "air bites
shrewdly; it is very cold," and "It is a nipping and an
eager air"?

Horatio: What does this mean, my lord?
Hamlet: The king doth wake to-night, and takes his rouse,
Keeps wassail, and the swaggering up-spring reels;
And, as he drains his draughts of Rhenish down,
The kettle-drum and trumpet thus bray out
The triumph of his pledge.
Horatio: Is it a custom?

Hamlet: Ay, marry, is't:
But to my mind,–though I am native here,
And to the manner born,–it is a custom
More honour'd in the breach than the observance.
This heavy-headed revel, east and west,
Makes us traduc'd and tax'd of other nations:
They clepe us drunkards, and with swinish phrase
Soil our addition; and, indeed, it takes
From our achievements, though perform'd at height,
And pith and marrow of our attribute.
So, oft it chances in particular men,
That, for some vicious mole of nature in them,
As, in their birth (wherein they are not guilty,
Since nature cannot choose his origin.)
By the o'er growth of some complexion,
Oft breaking down the pales and forts of reason;
Or by some habit, that too much o'er-leavens
The form of plausive manners;–that these men,–
Carrying, I say, the stamp of one defect,
Being nature's livery, or fortune's star,–
Their virtues else (be they as pure as grace,
As infinite as men may undergo,)
Shall in the general censure take corruption
From that particular fault: the dram of base
Doth all the noble substance often dout,
To his own scandal.

Who but Shakespeare could permit Othello in his last moment of life the serenity and sanity of such detachment as the following?

I have done the state some service, and they know 't;
No more of that. I pray you, in your letters,
When you shall these unlucky deeds relate,
Speak of me as I am; nothing extenuate,
Nor set down aught in malice: then, must you speak
Of one that lov'd not wisely but too well.

Othello

It is apparent that the stage and the study mutually enhance each other, and that neither separately nor together can they pluck the heart out of Shakespeare's mystery. We can, however, participate joyfully in mental, emotional, and spiritual experiences that we do not fully understand. The fringe benefits of Shakespeare's mind may become in part the fringe benefits of our own, and the rhythmic beat of the heart of his mystery may echo in our own.

This specially gifted poet, this superb craftsman of quality invites us to approach the mystery of things with humility and awe and not with the awful cunning of the social scientist. The home, the church, and the school have still much to learn from the creative artist whose intuitive insights lead to wisdom. Are they in any mood to learn, or must we continue to exclaim with Feste, the Clown, in *Twelfth Night*:

And thus the whirligig of time brings in his revenges?

2. *Shakespeare's Genius*

According to Holinshed's *Chronicles* (1582) Macbeth was a "cruel and intrepid man of action" and Duncan, a man of "soft and gentle nature." In Holinshed's brief account of the career of Macbeth, Shakespeare also discovered the "weird sisters" and their prophesies, the place called Dunsinane, and the names of Banquo, Macduff, and Malcolm.

In 1040 Duncan was murdered by Macbeth's assassins, murder being at that time a historically sanctioned passage to a throne, and Macbeth became the thane of "Glammis." In 1057 Macduff slew Macbeth in single combat, and Malcolm was crowned at Scone.

When Shakespeare's imagination began to play on these bare facts seventeen years of history were compressed into about seven days of dramatic action. He personalized history and created and delineated the characters of Macbeth, Banquo, the porter of hellgate, and the ghost of

Banquo. To the equivocations of the sisters he added hallucinatory themes. He contrasted Macbeth and Lady Macbeth as symbols of evil. The former interpreted omens as matters of fancy, and the latter as matters of fact. The former felt remorse but defied it, and the latter rejected the thought of penitence. Shakespeare traced the effects of surrender to habitual sin, created a sequence of conflicting morals and motives, and delineated Macbeth's and Lady Macbeth's degeneration to violent ends. Nature was contrasted with anti-nature, and time with expediency. Over the whole scene Shakespeare threw a blanket of gloom and silence, awful and pervading, pierced frequently by tantalizing flashes of light from swords and torches, horrifying screams of infants, weird incantations from witches, and the thunder of horses' hoofs.

In 1606 the play *Macbeth* was first produced in London. It is the shortest and most compact of Shakespeare's dramas. In the interaction of characters, morals, and motives it is the least complex. Shakespeare at the time was forty-two years of age.

No one has succeeded in plucking the heart out of Shakespeare's mystery. His genius remains an enigma, hidden in "the dark backward and abysm of time." He was the mouthpiece of his characters. By contrast the characters created by G. B. Shaw are often the mouthpieces of Shaw's opinions. Shakespeare's wisdom, on the other hand, was the equal of his genius.

3. *Frontiers of Wisdom*

Thomas Hardy summed up an item of his philosophy in the dictum "If way to the better there be, it exacts a good look at the worst." Hardy denied the charge of pessimism, and so should we. How is a better way to be discovered, if not by contrast and comparison with the worst?

What are a few of the conditions that beset or bedevil the classroom teacher? Like everyone else he lives in a world where violence may erupt at any time, where cruelty and meanness are rampant and where truculence and irresponsibility express the pride and vanity of those who assume a divine right to get what they want and to do as they please. The most childishly innocent exponents of this selfish impudence are the mini-minded young bulls and heifers that bellow the glamour of rebellion in an off-key. Against this clamour, the voice of the teacher represents the establishment, tradition, order, and organization. His behaviour is too seemly to be believed and his school too square to be real. How can he make himself heard?

His cause, however, is not lost. In spite of their bizarre behaviour, the bellicose beatniks have squandered good arguments through a failure to communicate effectively. Some of what they had to say needed saying, but now that their dedication has been diverted to destructive trips, their message has become unconvincing. Perhaps we have become immune to shock treatment. The rebels have succumbed to the security of the smug minority. The classroom teacher is still free, however, to express his own special brand of belief or doubt.

In one way or another we are all touched with madness. We are distinguishable from one another by either the kind or the degree of our oddity. On what authority dare anyone presume priority or sanity in all things? And this condition calls for patience, understanding, and sympathy with others in our common, creature predicament. It profits little to juxtapose extreme opinions with others just as violent. Love can outweigh hate if only by a narrow margin. The cacophony of the folk-singer sounds to him like eternity, but his universe is as temporary as a frog pond in midsummer. Why scream at tyranny? Why not cultivate a readiness to accept one another's mistakes at a discount? In our common lunacy a sense of humour is a saving grace. This is the beginning of wisdom within the law.

Thirty-five years ago the panacea of educational ills was forecast in "progressive education" with its programme of life adjustment, group acceptance, and amateur psychiatry. Through the years Deweyism and its ardent disciples have been denounced as a hoax and a fraud. Education, meanwhile, has rolled on, through, and over its own progressivism. Today another universal remedy is at hand. *Individually Prescribed Instruction* (I.P.I.) is now hailed by the director of research for the U.S. office of education as the greatest educational breakthrough of recent times. It promises individualized education for every child. Each youngster works at a different lesson. Everyone learns more. The top one-fourth will be well into college work by the time they finish high school. "I.P.I. requires vast quantities of materials for teachers to draw upon to fulfil the various learning needs of individual students. Teachers find out what the students need through constant testing: placement tests, pre-tests, tests imbedded in the materials, and post-tests. The materials, costly and difficult to develop, use a technique called programming. This involves presentation of a small amount of information to the student and then requiring him to make a response. It's devised so the student almost always gives the right response — and is told so immediately. Kids love it." Two obstacles lie in the way of its general use in the U.S.A. To this many a classroom teacher will reply "So here we go again!"

1. "The federal government would have to spend about four hundred million dollars a year for a number of years in this development."
2. "Every significant advance in educational practice must find its way past dozens of vested interests."

The classroom teacher is doubtless one of those vested interests. You will know that the moment of truth has arrived when you are no longer asked: What subject do you teach? but In what situation do you operate? When the pupil is no longer asked: What subject are you studying? but How are you being programmed?

It is fair to suspect, however, that the full implementation of I.P.I. will be deferred beyond the life-time of most of us.

In these schemes, unfortunately, there is little that is new. Many colleges and universities on this continent have for years been catering to the special needs of students who have selected their own areas of learning. Whether many pupils in elementary and secondary schools, graded or ungraded, are yet anxious and knowledgeable enough to make proper selections for their own needs is a problem that must be solved before programming begins. Can society afford to let young people waste their time seeking personal answers to primitive problems that mankind solved thousands of years ago? Must some problems be reworked pragmatically only to prove them workable? Has the widsom of the ages no longer any validity? The rugged common sense of the classroom teacher may still be the pupil's greatest challenge and consolation. WHO'S UP FRONT? may still determine the success of the learning process.

Reading the manifestos of some departments of educational research and graduate schools of education, one would think that the classroom teacher was a stupid ignoramus, without knowledge of individual differences, illiterate in the subject he teaches, unskilled in the techniques of teaching, and unaware of the shibboleths that confuse the innocent. The time is ripe to challenge the implications of those who aim to discredit the teacher. What are a few of the chief improvements made in education in the past forty years? The building of thousands of well-equipped schools; the enlarging of school districts; the vastly improved curricula offering a variety of options; spectacular developments in the study and practice of art, music, drama, physical education, social and physical sciences, mathematics, language, and literature. To these may be added expanded library services and an entirely new attitude of pupils to school and to education. Forty years ago only two teachers in the whole of Ontario were producing Shakespeare with high school casts. Today there are over two hundred. Forty years ago a high school orchestra was something unheard of. Today every school of moderate size has its corps of musical virtuosi. These improvements have been brought about through the combined efforts of teachers and principals, inspectors and superintendents, trustees and political leaders. To the educational enterprise reflected in these achievements the researchers and the professional theorists have contributed nothing. But these dropouts from the discipline of classroom teaching, these jargonauts of the educational space programme, still ride "piggy-back" on the system, and the cost of transporting them to their figure-factories of isolation in the mists of a never-never land is running into millions of dollars. And it must be remembered that research in education bears resemblance to research in the sciences in name only. The glamour and the prestige of the words *research* and *graduate* nevertheless overwhelm the mind. They cast a spell of platitudes too thick to penetrate. Viewing the mysterious exclusiveness and self-importance of these educational theorists and researchers from afar, the classroom teacher might be tempted to recite to his neighbour this morsel of wisdom from Emily Dickinson:

> "I'm nobody! Who are you?
> Are you nobody too?
> Then there's a pair of us!
> Don't tell! They'll banish us you know.

How dreary to be somebody!
How public–like a frog–
To tell your name the live-long June
To an admiring bog.

Among the most persistent phenomena of experience is the philanthropic zeal with which some people try to direct and control the lives of others. They presume to know better than others what is wrong in the realm of human affairs and how to correct it. In our time we have seen a succession of revolutions: communism, fascism, nationalism, individualism, and charters of human rights. And now the industrialists have got into the act. Observe the amount of "revolutionary hardware" in our "multimedia world" that is finding its way into the school: projectors and tape recorders, microfilm and duplicators, radio and motion pictures, television and computers. Subject courses, we are told, must be reconstructed to fit the *new media* in order to bring about the "explosive liberation of human intelligence," eliminate illiteracy, challenge the gifted, overcome teacher shortage, completely alter the learning process, and banish forever the time wasted in *doubting* and *questioning*. And all this is to be accomplished at one fell swoop. We have all heard most of it before.

Surely no one will deny that these machines of education, each in its own way, can transmit certain kinds of information quickly and effectively. These articles of educational hardware have power to expand our knowledge of many things in many ways. They should be employed wherever appropriate and possible.

A computer programmed to develop knowledge and skill in the use of grammatical forms, linguistic usages, metrical patterns, and literary technical terms will greatly assist the teacher in disposing of the garbage of educational materials. This in turn will leave the teacher free to extract the nourishing essences on which the mind of the pupil must feed to grow. These gadgets, for all their "tripe-ical" splendour, may challenge the teacher, but they cannot replace him. They have neither increased nor improved our knowledge of the learning process, but the teacher may do so if the pupil-teacher ratio is drastically reduced. The basic instrument of education is still the book. The central, indispensable figure in the school is still the classroom teacher. What can he do with the book, the software of education, that the movie screen or the programmed computer cannot do? He can show how inferences are made, consequences predicted and judged, values discovered and applied, and thought-processes managed. He may help pupils to gain insight into their own set of values, to initiate ideas, to participate effectively as a member of a group, and to resolve conflicting evidence. Among other things, he may lead his pupils to explore and sort out the differences between vanity and sanity, prejudice and principle, knowledge and wisdom, intellectual independence and intelligent cooperation, and between what is manifest and what is latent in literature, between what is in bad taste and what is in good taste in life.

At a time when mass media can provide so much information, both the teacher and the pupil may feel that they are being sucked down by an undertow and carried out to sea. Both may feel a loss of identity and a sense of belonging. Both may feel depersonalized and alienated from each other by the mass production process. There is another subtle danger posed by the computer. The programme may be confused with reality or mistaken for the pupil. If the pupil deferred to the computer's rather than to the teacher's decision, would fresh thought be stultified and learning destroyed? How will both the teacher and the pupil respond to being programmed? And in this rapidly expanding world of information what would happen if the pupil decided to modify the vagaries of the machine and enlarge the options available? Can the computer accommodate the perverse attractiveness of illogicality and irrationality that lurks in the human mind? A good teacher, on the other hand, encourages his pupils to outthink him and to make discoveries he has overlooked intentionally or otherwise. Since anyone who sets out to acquire an education is bound to suffer a "sea change" of one kind or another, a brain rinse is preferable to a brain wash.

In a classroom where a masterpiece of English literature is being read creatively, the pupil stands on the threshold of wisdom. His knowledge of the paraphernalia of the literary art may be increased but his capacity for wisdom will be expanded and deepened by literary experience, by his questioning of ideas and feelings, by his discovering of the unity hidden between contrasts, and by his comparing the experiences of others with his own. Knowledge will accrue to his powers of attention, perception, and persistence; wisdom will accumulate around his powers of imagination, retention, and reflection. Among the chief attributes of literary experience are the validity and indispensability of the imagination and the quality of the insights it so lavishly provides. Around it the student may organize his own value judgments concerning what is most worth-while in experience, and add new dimensions of significance to his own life.

Take, for example, Conrad's *Lord Jim*. The novelist probes problems in man's nature and fate and raises questions that the physical and social sciences ignore and that the philosopher and the theologian do not think to ask. Compare with the movie version of this masterpiece, your study of the text and estimate their respective values! Which left a shallow and which a deep and lasting impression on your mind? There is a place, nevertheless, for the movie version. Like a first general reading, it provides an excellent introduction to the intensive study of the text. And be assured that the intensive study is necessary if we are to meet the author on his own ground. Great art confronts us with some of the profoundest meanings of life. It brings what is deepest in our nature to the surface.

Or consider Shakespeare's *Hamlet* or *Henry V* when either is exposed to a class of students with little interest in reading and literature. Let them see the movie or better still the play itself performed at Stratford. Then engage them in a study of the text to see what it can add to their interest. Later distribute recordings of the famous speeches for student evaluations of interpretations. Finally with a student cast produce the drama for a paying audience. Shakespeare's plays are durable. They will survive any punishment. What makes his dramas so unique is the "massive integrity" of the man himself. His mind encompassed all phases of the artistic processes from insights into the tragic story of man's existence to the creation of characters and situations that can extract the essence of total response from an audience or a reader. No one, better than Shakespeare, perceived and portrayed the touch of madness in our creatureship. No one possessed a better mind for the accommodation of a great variety of ideas and images at one and the same time. No one could better integrate the significance of the parts with the meaning of the whole. No one understood better than Shakespeare that in all the arts, as in life itself, significance explodes in a vertical pattern rather than on a horizontal plane. The spontaneous thrust of a fountain is more exciting and revealing than the continuous flow of a river.

4. *"Time and the Hour"*

How does the creative reading of great literature advance the cause of wisdom in the reader? A brief passage from *Macbeth* will suffice. Here follows a summary of the questions asked, points discussed, speculations awakened, surmises reached, and discoveries made in a forty-minute les-

son with a senior class. In this intensive study we have
the advantage of knowing how the play ends, and can
take time to look backward and forward as through a tele-
scope on the whole action and to savour every morsel of
meaning that a small part of the drama, as an organic
integrated whole, can provide.

    Enter Lady Macbeth, reading a letter.
"They met me in the day of success; and I have learned by
the perfectest report, they have more in them than mortal
knowledge. When I burned in desire to question them
further, they made themselves air, into which they vanished.
Whiles I stood rapt in the wonder of it, came missives from
the King, who all-hailed me 'Thane of Cawdor'; by which
title, before, these weird sisters saluted me, and referred
me to the coming on of time with 'Hail, King that shalt
be!' This have I thought good to deliver thee, my dearest
partner of greatness, that thou mightest not lose the dues
of rejoicing by being ignorant of what greatness is promised
thee. Lay it to thy heart, and farewell."

                                        (Act i, Sc. v)

Why is it significant that on Lady Macbeth's first appearance
she is alone?

    The absence of an antecedent for "They" raises ques-
tions. Is this only part of the letter? Or is it one in a series?
Evidently Lady Macbeth realized at once to whom "They"
referred. Were this military general and his lady in constant
communication with each other by messenger? Evidence
from the sleep-walking scene gives proof that they were.
The Gentlewoman reports that again and again she
watched Lady Macbeth "take forth paper, fold it, write
upon't, read it, and afterwards seal it." What is thus
revealed of the relationship of these dearest partners of
greatness? How well do they know and trust each other?
Who depends on whom? Who defers to whom? What is
Macbeth's state of being? What is reflected of his attitude

in "They met me" rather than *I met them*? Why does he
fix the time as "the day of success"? How does he try to
convince Lady Macbeth that the witches are good omens
for both of them? Why does he set such store by the supernatural by implying that the witches have "immortal"
knowledge? Why should he take pains to report this to
Lady Macbeth? "When I burned in desire" says Macbeth:
what was burning him up? What "further" did he wish
to know? And what does this tell us of the nature of his
mind? Did the witches make themselves a screen of air
or mist, or did they transform themselves into air? Which
did Macbeth mean? "Whiles I stood rapt": What was the
cause of his rapture? Why did the confirmation of the
witches' prophecy set his imagination on fire? It was further
proof that natural events and supernatural destiny were
combined. Macbeth was impressed because he wanted to
be. The weird (wyrd) sisters were, he believed, omens of
a benevolent fate. Did he deliberately withhold from Lady
Macbeth his knowledge that Duncan was on his way and
that the Prince of Cumberland had been named the King's
successor, or was his mind completely consumed by the
fact that the witches had sought him out? From Lady Macbeth's immediate response to the letter, we may assume
that she was well acquainted with his moody spells, and
had to steel herself to overthrow his qualms of conscience
and his scruples. Were his reasons for informing her
feigned or real? Some critics have assumed that Lady Macbeth was to complete the work that the witches had begun,
but this is inconsistent with the facts as Shakespeare has
revealed them. The witches were quite capable of carrying
out their own machinations in their own peculiar way. Lady
Macbeth was not a witch. She would not vanish into thin
air as they had done, and she would not refuse to confer
with Macbeth as they had done. Like Macbeth, she was
a human being and subject to the frailties of human nature.
The fate of both was embedded in their own minds and

thought-processes. Neither one could wait for time to run its course. Both were obsessed by an evil spirit of expeditious zeal.

The witches had referred Macbeth to "the coming on of time," but with his mind befogged by his own exultation, he could not wait for time to fulfil their prophecy. He must make his own time. He must make time his servant. Here lies a tragic flaw in his nature and character. There had been a time when as a free man and an honoured leader he could say "*Time* and the hour runs through the roughest day." But once he failed to heed the witches' reference to "the coming on of *time*," time began to set in motion its revenge. "To beguile the *time*, Look like the *time*" counseled Lady Macbeth. She, too, would cheat time. Later we hear the Porter of hellgate call out to his guests "Come in time," meaning right on time, or all come this way in good time.

> I had thought to have let in some of all professions, that go the primrose way to the everlasting bonfire.

As Macbeth contemplates the destruction of Macduff's castle and family, he says "*Time*, thou anticipatest my dread exploits." He failed to foresee that a time would come when sick at heart, hag-haunted, without friends, and Lady Macbeth dead

> She should have died hereafter
> There would have been a *time* for such a deed

time no longer would have any significance for him. Lady Macbeth would have created time, but time cheated her of life by death before her natural time.

> Tomorrow, and tomorrow, and tomorrow,
> Creeps in this petty pace from day to day,
> To the last syllable of recorded *time*.

Macbeth had taken it upon himself to expedite the prophecy of the witches, and now his expediency has gone down to defeat before the battering ram of *time*, and he himself has been cast aside as a disillusioned creature with no one left to turn to but the witches:

> I will tomorrow,
> And *betimes* I will, to the weird sisters.

By seeking their help when all hopes had been borne away on "the sightless couriers of the air," he plumbed the depth of degradation. How villainously had they juggled with his fate!

> If you can look into the seeds of *time*
> And say which grain will grow and which will not,
> Speak then to me.

Macbeth was a gambler who in order to win would turn the moral world of nature upside down and invite the fiendish forces of anti-nature to come in.

> . . .that but this blow
> Might be the be-all and the end-all here,
> But here, upon this bank and shoal of *time*,
> We'ld jump the life to come.

Tricked by the equivocations of the devil, he later pleaded that some power might "take the present horror from the *time*" instead of bringing more "new hatch'd to the woful *time*" to plague him.

> Had I but died an hour before this chance
> I had lived a blessed *time*.

Even now he felt no remorse for the murders he had committed. They were all a part of "a blessed time." The witches had made a fool of him, and now in desperation he defied their hideous jests. He could no longer be their monster,

And live to be the show and gaze o' the *time*.

But time would no longer be beguiled.

The night is long that never finds the day.

The measured pace of time had moved too slowly for Macbeth, but in the end it was time that overwhelmed him.

In the light of all that may be inferred from this discussion, suppose that Macbeth had for some time previous to the opening of the drama contemplated the demise of the King! Suppose that Macbeth had grown impatient with Duncan's senility and fulsome courtesies! If he had for some time planned somehow to dispose of the King, what light would these suppositions throw on our interpretations? How would they affect the dimensions of the torture chamber of Macbeth's mind where daggers flashed and dripped with "gouts of blood"? And what further speculations does this thought awaken concerning Macbeth's pride, vanity, remorse, and fear of retribution for his crimes?

It certainly was not beyond the capacity of Shakespeare's mind to accommodate all these possibilities, and they add a great deal to Shakespeare's dramatic portrait of Macbeth and to our study of the man. Or was Macbeth one of Shakespeare's "villians by necessity, fools by heavenly compulsion" as referred to in *King Lear* (Act i, Sc. ii). Great art leaves some problems unresolved because they are insoluble. All our lives we participate in truth without recognizing it or realizing its implications. We are all slow learners and in need of wise and patient teachers who have time to deal with our peculiar problems.

It is also worth noting that Macduff at birth had been "*untimely*" ripped." Even at Macbeth's death, *time* was still taking its revenge on the impostor who dared to ring its changes. "Truth is the daughter of time" says an old proverb.

The play *Macbeth* belongs in the realm of vision, Macbeth's vision of a prophecy, Lady Macbeth's vision of a promise, and Shakespeare's vision of their obsession with the fulfilment of their visions. As we observe the drama unfolding, we apprehend a vision of the mind's potential for evil and of the degradation to which the human spirit can descend. We, too, have become absorbed by the tragedy of two creatures who, not unlike ourselves, have become enmeshed in a tangled web of their own weaving and have lost the free will necessary to extricate themselves from the coils of an evil course. The irony of the situation lay in the fact that the results of their precipitous action only time would tell.

In that lesson the class may have made a discovery that the critics of three hundred years have overlooked, namely Macbeth's contest with time and its consequences. What better confirmation is required of the wisdom that may accrue to the practice of creative reading?

Dag Hammerskjöld left behind in his *Markings* a statement that might be read as a commentary on *Macbeth*:

> You cannot play with the animal in you without becoming wholly animal, play with falsehood without forfeiting your right to truth, play with cruelty without losing your sensitivity of mind. He who wants to keep his garden tidy doesn't reserve a plot for weeds.

The effect of this morsel of wisdom *on* the mind is quite harmless when compared with the effect *in* the mind of the drama or the fiction or the poem that involves the reader in a total commitment.

What are some of the attributes of wisdom that may be seen in action or in conflict with their opposites in the pages of literary masterpieces? Courage and fortitude, honesty and generosity, patience and tolerance, perseverance and prudence, modesty and humility are all products of the spirit, and the spirit is the breath of the soul. This assumption eliminates from consideration the plethora of *Whodunits* on the market today. They are chiefly concerned with solving plots not persons, with finding the weapon not the motive. They add little to our better understanding of our fellow man. It is the man of reason living in a community of faith, striving against irrationality and folly, triumphing over barbarism and superstition, trying to preserve an ideal in the midst of the real, poking fun at panoplied chaos and ideological disorder, and expressing his visions and values in works of art with imagination, insight, and compassion who is the hero in the tragic story of man's existence on earth. For proof one need look no farther afield than the acknowledged masterpieces of literary art.

5. *"The Play's the Thing"*

Once upon a time, according to Hans Christian Andersen, there dwelt in the dark woods of ancient China a nightingale that sang so sweetly that its song could melt to tears the stony hearts of men. It became a favourite with the emperor and a fashion with his courtiers to wait upon the pleasure of this gifted singer. Men came from afar to hear it sing and to spread its fame abroad. Even the emperor of Japan came and was so impressed that he had his technicians make him a mechanical nightingale that, when wound up with a key, would play one little tune over and over again. It was an ingenious imitation of the real nightingale. This he sent as a gift to the emperor of China. Mechanical nightingales soon became a vogue, and they set up such a clatter in the land that the real nightingale flew away and was heard no more in the gardens of the emperor.

In recent years a variety of mechanical aids has been introduced into the schools at considerable expense to the taxpayers. It appears, by the way, that funds are always available for machines and equipment but seldom for a reduction in the pupil-teacher ratio. Television sets, record players, movie projectors, and tape recorders, along with a plethora of ancillary gadgets, are expected eventually to replace the textbook and turn the teacher into a classroom technician. It is not to be inferred from this comment that every mechanical device is worthless or that every teacher can sing like a nightingale, but anything that interferes with the free flow of ideas between a teacher and a student or between students and students in the normal teaching and learning situation in a classroom delays and diverts the impact of the educative process. It becomes not an aid but a hindrance.

Evidence is already available that students are growing weary of the use of educational hardware. Television is no longer a novelty; in fact, it can be a bore! It cannot wait upon response! The printed word, on the other hand, is always there as a frame of reference unless the teacher, taking his cue from an erudite editor, activates his mechanical nightingale as he does in this brief analysis:

> Hence! home, you idle creatures, get you home.
> Is this a holiday? What! know you not,
> Being mechanical, you ought not walk
> Upon a labouring day without the sign
> Of your profession? Speak, what trade art thou?
> > *Julius Caesar*, Act 1, Scene 1

Does *idle* in this context mean lazy, unemployed, or emptyheaded? (See notes) What is the opposite of *holiday*? (labouring day) How did the opposite of a working-day come to be called a holiday? Refer to your dictionaries. (holy day) What is the meaning of *mechanical*? (a mechanic, a working man, according to the dictionary a man who works with the tools of a handicraft) *Ought not walk* means ought not (to) walk. This is the only occasion on which Shakespeare omits "to" after ought. What would be a *sign*, say, of a carpenter? (a hammer or saw) What must have been the custom then among working men on working days? (to carry with them in the street some mark of their trade). But there is no proof that any such law or custom prevailed in either Rome or London. We cannot be sure why Shakespeare began his play in this way. Now put the whole speech in your own words, paraphrase it.

There chatters the mechanical nightingale. You can hear the click, clack, clatter of the mechanism as the key of erudition winds it up and the springs of simplification wind it down. Shakespeare's text is turned into a source of various types of word-study and an exercise in paraphrasing. Of what value is all this learning (and the character-sketching and plot-building that go with it) if the pupil remains unmoved by the drama and unaware of the poetry? Must everything be understood to be enjoyed? Experience proves it otherwise! Many people who could not distinguish between a flute and a clarinet have found pleasure and profit listening to a symphony orchestra. We know very little about the meaning of life, and yet we all participate in it with zeal and vigour. We have all found satisfaction on occasion in many things that we have not completely understood, from Greek drama to modern fiction. We may not apprehend what truth is, or accept another's criterion of beauty, or comprehend the meaning of love, but we can all participate in all these things and grow wiser and more mature in the process. Why not let our pupils hear the real nightingale and participate with Shakespeare in his song? Why not stage-centre rather than page-centre the study of drama? Instead of translating the play word for word, like a passage of Latin prose, into the pupils' intelligences, produce the play by projecting it into their imaginations. Replace the "construe" method by the "production" method. It is amazing how words come alive in action and how much intuitive feeling and rich and warm understanding flow through the veins of the poetry when dramatically spoken. Words are not thus rendered less important than heretofore, but rather more important. Their connotation, as in all great literature, assists in determining their denotation. Intuitively the mind transcends the words without losing touch with them. It is in the light and warmth of the imagination that meaning and understanding are seared into consciousness. Without the imagination all is drudgery and dross.

> By logic and reason we die hourly; by imagination we live.
> J. B. Yeats, *Letters to his Son W. B. Yeats and Others*

In the study of great art there is more potential energy in fusion than in fission, the fusion of the pupil's mind with the poet's rather than in the fragmentation of a masterpiece into innumerable vaguely related parts the better to understand the parts. Is the meaning to be found in the separate parts or in the parts combined into a whole? Which is the shadow and which the substance? Where sings the real nightingale?

How does the "production" method function? After a first rapid reading of the play is completed, an attempt is made by means of discussion to ascertain its theme, to sense the depth, mystery, and wonder of the forest rather than to examine the foliage of different sorts of trees. Complete agreement may be impossible to reach. It is unnecessary so long as every one thinks his way through to some kind of tentative overall meaning of the drama, to something like a play-director's working brief. To illustrate this point, a class might decide to produce Shakespeare's *Julius Caesar* as a play about power, and assume that all the main characters in the drama have nibbled on the insane root of lust for power. From beginning to end an evil spirit broods over the action and drives men to their doom. The source of this evil is in the hearts of men, in the frailties of their human nature, in the smugness of Caesar, the jealousy of Cassius, the pride and vanity of Brutus, the stupidity of Casca, and the cunning of Antony. Caesar, the self-styled superman, with much evidence of god-like strength and human weakness to support his claim, would found a dynasty to perpetuate his greatness. The envious Cassius worships in himself the very power and authority that he hates in other men. His ambition ends in the appeasing of his private griefs. He would probably not know what to do with an empire if he had one. The high-minded Brutus dreams of a state in which:

> Ambition's debt is paid.

In the name of abstract justice and speculative reason Brutus fights a private war to end all wars and unwittingly but philosophically lays the foundations for a civil war. Casca is no comic fool. He is a respectable officer of state, perhaps the captain of the Consular Guard. He is the type of administrative officer that Shakespeare loved to lampoon. He is a trimmer, desperately anxious to be on the winning side, miserably fearful of his own skin. Casca is a forerunner of Polonius. Antony was the devoted protégé of Caesar while Caesar lived to satisfy his vain ambition for prestige, but once the beloved Caesar was no more, Antony looked about him. He found an empire ready for the taking, something to be had on the cheap, a challenge to the wily skill of a gambler who could beguile the people. Antony was loyal to Caesar and his memory, but deceitful to the people. To serve his own ends, he used the very mob that he despised:

> Nay, press not so upon me; stand far off.

In one way or another all these men sought personal power, and the cause of their failure may be summed up in a paraphrase of Cassius' famous observation:

> The fault dear Brutus is not in our stars
> But in ourselves, that we have tragic faults.

Yet all these men were "loving" friends. They belonged to the same club, subscribed to the same convenient superstitions, and carried the same daggers hidden on their persons. Their women shopped in the same markets and agitated the same social column. But if *Julius Caesar* is a picture of Roman life in a certain period of history, it is a poor one. *Julius Caesar* is not a picture, but a problem – a problem that is everywhere. And because Shakespeare read life as well as his Plutarch, he may easily have found the problem among his contemporaries, the poets, playwrights, patrons, and politicians of his own time – even among the men of his own company of players. Rome, like Illyria, he found sufficiently remote and imaginatively appealing to be impersonal, but the cobbler in the opening scene is certainly an Englishman and not a Roman.

With some such director's brief in mind the class is prepared to discuss the production and engage in the dramatic reading and performance of the play. Without this overall point of view, which usually is seldom discussed or even considered and is never mentioned in the texts, the parts have little meaning in a created living situation, the significant words have only minor importance, and the whole play disintegrates into a series of vaguely related fragments. Shakespeare's *Julius Caesar* is not a historical document, a philosophical treatise, a moral preachment, or a story with a message. It is a drama that moves us because it contains something of the power that animates all creation. It flows rapidly and smoothly along from one phase or pattern of action into another, not in a horizontal plane like blocks laid end to end, but in a vertical pattern like blocks piled one on top of another. The horizontal plane leads the mind away from the central theme – from the saturated whole to the fragmented parts. The vertical pattern embraces the intangibles. Every pattern of action, whether it be four lines or forty, is essential to the whole, and some of them are epitomes of the whole. And through the drama, holding it erect and giving it meaning, runs the spinal theme remarkable for its integrity and variety of intensity. It is this theme, this meaning, that each student apprehends in varying degrees as he experiences the drama. It is this that enlarges the scope of his mind, stimulates and purifies his imagination, and deepens his sense of wonder. It is this that he feels and remembers because it is the source and cause of the change that the experiencing of the drama makes within him. Each pattern or phase of action has its lesser theme that contributes to the accumulative effect of the whole; and the drama should be studied or rehearsed by means of these patterns rather than by long and complicated scenes arbitrarily determined by ingenious editors.

Now let us turn again to the first scene of *Julius Caesar*. It provides more than a glimpse of the contrasts and conflicts that are to follow. It consists of three patterns of action, first the bear-baiting of Marullus by the commoners, second the contrast between the bombastic rhetoric of Marullus and the restrained eloquence of Flavius, and then the shockingly ambitious plans of Flavius, a tribune, to clip Caesar's wings. Now apply to these patterns of action the production method. Cast a tall boy of commanding appearance to represent Flavius, a short, stocky, bumptious lad to be Marullus, the clown in the class to interpret the second commoner, and any nondescript, indifferent fellow to speak for the first commoner. The pupils themselves can assist in the casting. The remainder of the class, who may very well remain in their seats, become members of the mob. They laugh and shout their approval of the second commoner's wit, and throughout Marullus' oration, praising the memory of Pompey and reprimanding the people, they oppose him with their shouts and clamours. Why should they not? They have confessed themselves in favour of Caesar who can keep them on a comfortable dole – a form of civil service list. Let us suppose that the first reading is feeble and hopeless. Now discuss the rehearsal of the action, seeking better stage positions at the front of the room, better gestures, attitudes, tones, and more significant interpretations of the key passages. It is not enough merely to read the play. In the reading it must be acted out either in the imagination or on stage. The sharp contrast between Flavius and Marullus soon becomes apparent. The contrasting attitudes of the commoners towards the two tribunes, respecting the one, despising the other, appear natural and obvious, because these attitudes are inseparable from the very words of the text when they are heard as well as seen, and seen in action.

How trite, pedantic, and remote from dramatic experience now seems the aimless chatter about *idle, holiday, mechanical, ought walk*, etc. etc. Their meanings become instantly obvious in the action and the dramatic reading when the right words, not the wrong ones, come to the surface and force themselves on the attention. If a pupil does not sense the amusement that springs from the cobbler's punning, let another pupil who does feel it explain it. Let the meaning of words be worked out from their context. That is what an audience does, and what we do when we read. That is what our pupils do at the movies, in front of the television screen, and in the street. They, too, want most of all to read life, even as Shakespeare did, to read life and explore its problems and unanswerable riddles. Eighty per cent of our pupils have no interest whatever in what might be called scholarship in literary matters, but nearly all of them love a good story, exciting conflicts and dramatic action. There is nothing precious or exclusive about such delights. They will find all of these elements in Shakespeare if they are allowed to read and rehearse his plays as plays. They will, moreover, never forget the experience, if we meet these young people where they are in their needs and not where we think they should be on our sophisticated scale of literary values. It is sometimes suspected that as teachers we have become too smart and too academic.

Discuss the direction and production of this opening action, rehearse it, set up competing casts, let girls try the parts of Flavius and Marullus and the second commoner, and Shakespeare's genius will live again in the minds of the pupils, his plays will begin to come alive, and his famous personages will walk down the street, not stand transfixed in print like tailor's dummies in a store window.

If when this first action is over the pupils feel that here lies the basis for violent conflicts to come, that society is in a sad state of affairs, that everybody is selfish and anxious only to satisfy his personal vanity or greed, that the common people are likely to suffer for the sins of their leaders, that the introduction of modest reforms is past hoping for, and that they want to rehearse the next series of actions, if they feel like this, the production method has been a success. The pupils will have participated in some of the experience that the Elizabethan audience enjoyed.

What at first, according to the construe method, appeared to be the solid substance of Shakespearean study has become unreal and less than a shadow, and the shadowy essence of the drama has begun to cast its outlines on the screen of the imagination. Harken! the real nightingale has begun again to sing in the deep foliage of Shakespeare's "verbal delirium."

Hardly is the threat of Flavius heard:

> These growing feathers pluck'd from Caesar's wing
> Will make him fly an ordinary pitch.

than the mighty eagle swoops upon us with all his feathers flying. His first command is to his wife; his second to his young lieutenant. Caesar must have an heir as well as a triumph–a triumph to which he was not entitled–and his concern with both is tied into the Lupercal, a popular religious festival, the feast of fertility. Truly this Caesar hath become a god–at least in the eyes of his envious friends who noted carefully the obsequious behaviour of the loving, fawning Antony whose "quick spirit" offended Brutus.

The production method applied to this unit of action is most revealing. To decide on the stage positions of all these people, the elite of the civilized world, their relation to one another, their deportment, their manual and verbal rhetoric, provides an intensely interesting and valuable exercise in the study of human nature, in the use of the imagination, and in the sensitizing of the mind to the power latent in words. What further proof need be sought of their awareness of Shakespeare's dramatic insight and artistic economy? The play's the thing wherein to catch the conscience of the class.

Then over this brief scene of magnificence and power Shakespeare threw a pall of impending peril. Shrill and ominous comes the warning:

> Beware the Ides of March.

Five simple words, but they are full of foreboding. How should they be spoken on each occasion that they are heard? How should the part of the soothsayer be managed? How should the principal people on the stage react to him and to his words? How can the mystery latent in the exclamations and anxious enquiries be used to heighten the tension? Caesar is noticeably disturbed and tries to dissemble his anxiety by a peremptory dismissal of the soothsayer as a dreamer. How should he do this to convey the impression that he is a man of quick and decisive action? In the midst of this excitement Brutus and Cassius make their first speeches and reveal themselves fully and at once. Both men are concerned with the soothsayer. Where should they stand? What should they do? And how should they speak? Brutus, the Stoic, in dispassionate but slightly disdainful tones reports to Caesar:

A soothsayer bids you beware the Ides of March.

It is deeply ironical that he and not Casca, the master of ceremonies, should pick up and pass on this warning. For the rest of Brutus' life this warning is never far from his mind as is shown later on the eve of the assassination, on the battlefield, and at the hour of his death. On the other hand, Cassius, the Epicurean, anxious to get on to more useful matters, excalims:

Fellow, come from the throng; look upon Caesar.

The rhythms of the two men are in sharp contrast, the one smooth and measured, the other staccato and impulsive. Brutus and Cassius with their contrasting minds, beliefs, and ambitions are laid bare in seventeen plain words; and most of them are Saxon monosyllables and all are cast in the rhythm of natural and familiar speech. The rehearsal of this little unit or pattern of action never fails to engage the attention of the whole class and to involve them all in discussion. It deepens insight into both life and literature, and the pupils discover that they have powers of judgment and decision that they did not know they possessed. They become confident and more mature as the action develops.

The world of Shakespeare's creative imagination often seems more real than the world in which we live. He keeps us aware of life by reminding us of its accidents. Just before the assassination, for instance, Popilius Lena, passing by Cassius, drops a casual remark:

> I wish your enterprise today may thrive.

Who has not at some time been startled by some casual or apparently innocent remark? Why should this remark be made to Cassius of all people? What a chain of suspicions it awakens? What suicidal terror it evokes from Cassius? "Casca, be sudden," but will he be sudden enough? Here surely is proof sufficient that these lines must be acted out if their dramatic significance is to be imagined and apprehended. Cassius at this moment must be seen as well as heard. We must participate with Shakespeare and *learn by being* Cassius at least in our imaginations. Not the big words in Shakespeare but the little ones are often laden with intended meaning. Heard in the context of the dramatic action when verbal and manual rhetoric automatically enhance each other, the significant words become real and begin to sing. They fall "shrewdly to the purpose."

Cassius:	I think we are too bold upon your rest:
	Good morrow, Brutus; do we trouble you?
Brutus:	I have been up this hour, awake all night.
	Know I these men that come along with you?
Cassius:	Yes, every man of them; and no man here
	But honours you; and every one doth wish
	You had but that opinion of yourself
	Which every noble Roman bears of you.
	This is Trebonius.
Brutus:	He is welcome hither.

Cassius: This, Decius Brutus.
Brutus: He is welcome too.
Cassius: This, Casca; this, Cinna;
And this, Metellus Cimber.
Brutus: They are all welcome.
What watchful cares do interpose themselves
Betwixt your eyes and night?
Cassius: Shall I entreat a word?
(Brutus and Cassius whisper)
Decius: Here lies the east: doth not the day break here?
Casca: No.
Cinna: O! pardon, sir, it doth; and yon grey lines
That fret the clouds are messengers of day.
Casca: You shall confess that you are both deceiv'd.
Here, as I point my sword, the sun arises;
Which is a great way growing on the south,
Weighing the youthful season of the year.
Some two months hence up higher toward the north
He first presents his fire; and the high east
Stands, as the Capitol, directly here.

Act II, Sc. I

This unit of action, studied as if it were a piece of prose revealing a further development in the plot, offers no difficulty in language or understanding. Brutus and Cassius go into a huddle, and the rest of the conspirators engage in a childish dispute concerning the point at which the sun arises. In the conventional treatment of Shakespeare very little more than a discussion of these two points is ever undertaken.

Treated as a unit of dramatic action, however, with young actors to assist the imaginations of themselves and their audience, the scene awakens a sense of urgency, of doom and violent destiny, and of the inevitable results of desperate acts. The tones are all ominous. Brutus, haggard and worn by night-long vigil, is restless and indecisive. Cassius, still driven by his envy of Caesar and his power, still scheming with the single-minded earnest of a fiend, comes to apply new pressure on Brutus in the night. Pressure must never be relaxed. Cassius' timing of his visit is perfect. The atmosphere is tense with conspirational zeal and stealth. Hooded men and veiled disguise intensify the drama and the mystery. Who are these men? What do they look like? How do they behave? How do they approach Brutus when introduced? Is Casca pompous and swaggering? Is Cimber fawning or hypocritical? The scene is alive with action. Cassius, the real leader, still must call Brutus aside and whisper with him, and we are left to guess the nature of this conversation. This whispering contrasts sharply with the noisy argument of the others. A double disaster is impending − one for Caesar, the other for the conspirators. The grouping, the gestures, and the tones of voice associated with each speech collectively produce the effect intended. Even the non-speaking parts have a function. The action must be seen as the words are heard if the drama is to be lived through. The turmoil intensifies the irony. In the darkness-visible of this springtime dawn, swords point in all directions, and Casca, who is destined to be the first to strike at Caesar, points in the direction of the Capitol. Shakespeare is alive, and his text is only a script or sound-track. The pupils take away a memorable experience that will cleave to them for the rest of their lives.

Many of the notes supplied in the average text are not only useless but misleading and deceptive. They lead away into a form of erudition that has nothing to do with drama. They are often obstacles to production and to the apprehension of the real meaning of the play. Read life rather than the notes, read life first and always and the literature will then be more intelligible. We will then get at the heart of a text more quickly and easily. Pupils trained in the production method know the play far better than those trained in the construe method. They have penetrated more deeply into its real meaning and they better understand the parts in relation to the whole. They do not leave the classroom confused by an abundance of un-related snippets of information. They have felt a little of the singular impact of a powerful drama of human action. If possible, take the students to the theatre or to a movie or television screen to see *Julius Caesar,* or to the record player to hear it spoken, and urge them to discuss the merits and the limitations of such presentations, but far better is it to help the pupils to produce the play in the classroom for themselves. Even a feeble rendering of the play is better than none at all, provided the pupils are encouraged to identify themselves in imagination with these characters in this concentrated, intense, and life-like action. One of the best renderings I have ever heard of one of Shylock's famous speeches was given by an eleven-year old Jewish boy whose feelings quite transcended the notes in the margin of the text.

Given a chance to work with Shakespeare, pupils can teach one another a great deal. It is not too much to say that these young classroom actors can apprehend a new experience that may be akin to what Shakespeare left crys-tallized in words. Young pupils love to act. They do it naturally, and, left alone, will invent a world of make-believe. They may on occasion help the poet to sharpen sympathetic insight into the problems of existence and deepen intuitive understanding of life. They may learn as actors to work *with* us, the audience, and not *on* us, or *for* us, or *for* themselves. They may suddenly realize that Shakespeare breathed the life of individuality into his characters, that they all speak not in his language but in their own words, images, and metaphors. He despised none; he pitied all. They may perceive that it is the lust for power that turns these major characters in *Julius Caesar* into tragic figures. They may begin to suspect that the forum, the senate house, Sardis, and Philippi, can be found in miniature in many school-yards and classrooms and factories and offices today where all these characters have their counterparts. Given a chance the pupils will seldom mistake the shadow for the substance in either life or literature. They are quick to detect the difference between the real nightingale and the mechanical one. And, furthermore, if all studies in English, in both literature and composition, were approached in the same realistic way, beginning with the pupil where he is and helping him to grow up and mature by participating in the thoughts and feelings of the masters, living and learning might become synonymous terms.

Shakespeare was one of the few great dramatic poets of all time. We do his memory a disservice if we put his works on a literary pedestal and worship him from afar like a god. He was of our common humanity, of this good green earth, and he still invites us to see, hear, feel, and imagine life with his mind, on his terms, and in his words. It is our privilege as teachers to lead our pupils into the green pastures that he has prepared for us, but it is not our right to eat all the grass ourselves.

Current Educational
Contentions

1. *"Cabin'd, cribb'd, confin'd"*

In a recent article on psychology human beings were classified in one of a half-dozen categories as psychotics,
psychosomatics, neurotics, defectives, alcoholics, or paraly-
tics. If such classification were applied in the classroom,
the need for teaching would be at an end, and provided
the teachers were not replaced by sociologists, the nation
might soon have a host of geniuses in the arts and sciences.
We like things neat, definite, quick, complete, and final.
That is one of the reasons that the detective story, with
its problems solved completely and finally within its own
set terms, has such a wide appeal. It appeases the hunger
to know something whether it is worth knowing or not.
Its popularity is a symptom of the pragmatic state of mind.
It deadens the sense of wonder, and arouses speculation
and curiosity in puzzle solving. Assuming that all questions
are answerable, we want answers, swift and sure, slick and
shiny.

By contrast the "X marks the spot" feature is almost
negligible in the great fictions where the artist is concerned
with the creation of an imaginary world peopled by created
characters who are variations of ourselves. A masterpiece
of imaginative literature, like the human being, is unique!

It may be classified with others according to size or form but not according to its quality or spirit. Shakespeare's dramas, for instance, are distinct and differ sharply from one another in character and intention. Shakespeare presented some of the riddles of human existence but, true and great artist, he did not attempt to solve them. His plays raise many questions that are left unanswered. That is one of the major reasons why they still make good theatre. It is also a reason why they keep rolling off the shelf to say new things to every new generation of readers. They refuse to be shelved.

But why this zeal to have things and people classified, and labelled? Is it done to satisfy our desire to manage them, to sum them up, as it were, to dismiss them, to render them unreal? Years ago the education administrators introduced into this country the study of vocational guidance as a formal subject to compete with other subjects in a programme already congested. Today young people are more confused and undecided about themselves and their careers than ever before. Square pegs have not been kept out of round holes. Accepting human nature for what it is, it is doubtful if they ever can be! Too many uncontrollable factors are involved, and the guider often adds to the confusion. And now the cry goes up for more supervisors. A large sum of money, a gift from the Kellogg Foundation, has been set aside for the training of this special breed of educator. "Teachers are already 'supervised to death' by people who read books on education written by other people lacking experience in actual teaching." Nothing will kill good teaching more quickly than too much supervision. It should be remembered, however, that guidance and supervision often provide work for people who cannot or wish not to teach in a classroom. The pupils gain where the system loses.

A basic requisite of good teaching is a sense of freedom,

and freedom thrives in a soil of personal responsibility. An honest ideal worth aiming at would be to let the teacher fit his own course to the needs of his pupils, and then set his own examinations. If that were generally done, people would be amazed at the degree of uniformity that would prevail in such diversity and the prestige of the teacher in the community would rise noticeably. When the high school teacher enjoys some of the same kind of freedom of thought and action that the university teacher possesses, mutual respect will be secure. But if the teacher feels that he is being "typed" and graded and thrown into a melting pot of common statistical data, if he feels that he is being standardized, preserved, and rendered innocuously functional, the spectre of tin cans and cardboard cartons clouds his vision. His attitude goes sour, and his pupils know it. Their sense of freedom and feeling of responsibility are sharply curtailed. Education that could be alive and liberating becomes restrictive and confining. The whole meaning of discipline, as well as of education, is distorted.

> Our little systems have their day;
> They have their day and cease to be.
> – Tennyson *In Memoriam*

Few people today would deny that we have crossed the threshold of a new era in human history. A source of new and abundant energy has been revealed to man and the power to control and use it is rapidly being released to him He is a bold person who would hazard a guess concerning what the next hundred, or even the next ten, years may bring. Some things, however, are already known. The possession of atomic energy has already begun to change our thinking and feeling about man and nature. Imagine the further impact it will have on our way of life when someone discovers a cheap and easy method of shielding the user. Education is likely to become much more realistic, selective, and less tolerant of pulp. A new way of life is bound to force a re-examination of first principles in education.

What are some signs of disintegration in education today? The emphasis on the social at the expense of the educational values of schooling has run its course and has reached a dead end. Most pupils live their real lives outside the classroom. In spite of all the subjects offered nothing seems to absorb the whole attention of the pupil; the connection between his learning and his life seems to him to be remote. A true story may help to clarify this point.

In a small school in eastern Ontario, a boy, big for his age, sat sullenly in the back of the classroom. Try as she would the young teacher could not interest him in her subject. He made no trouble, but he did as little as possible and that unwillingly. At her wits' end she decided on a personal interview, and at the end of the day they met at her desk and sat down to talk things over. He was a hard nut to crack but she hammered away, and at last this story came out. He had run away from home and had joined the R.C.A.F. in Toronto. All went well until his parents discovered his whereabouts and disclosed his age. The commanding officer released him with the request that he return when of age since he was just the type he wanted. His father put him back to school, and here he was patiently waiting for his next birthday. He did not want to bother the teacher, and he hoped she would not bother him. Then her brain went to work, and things began to happen. If you are the kind of boy, she said, that the R.C.A.F. officer took you to be and that I think you are, you will not be content to be a member of a ground crew. Who knows but that some day, and that not far away, you may be a squadron leader, a person in command of others, in a place of authority, with great personal responsibilities! Who knows but that you may have to write letters to the parents of boys who didn't come back? What a duty that will be and what a test of your skill in the use of language! At that task you would not wish to fail. Well, language is my business and I can help you to write well if you care to learn. The rest of the story is obvious. She could not give him too much work to do. His whole attitude changed, and schooling and learning for the first time in his life took on a personal meaning.

Here was a completely successful encounter of two young people, full of heart and mind and spirit. It reminds one of Christ's method of teaching. It was a genuine test of the education process at the only level worth talking about, the level of pupil and teacher when two minds confront each other. That is the point at which the fission and fusion take place. It was creative teaching and far removed from the interference of either vocational guidance or supervision as they are so often and so pompously conceived. It reveals a young teacher's sympathetic insight into a pupil's problem and her imaginative understanding of a real situation. In part its effectiveness depended on the proper use of the right words in a living context.

Another weakness of contemporary education is its fragmentation. Parts are stressed at the expense of wholes, the parts becoming isolated and unreal, and the method formal and inflexible. Educational jargon becomes a counterfeit for thought, and the reading of educational documents a substitute for imaginative literature. The very sources of excellence in thought, feeling, and imagining are dammed up in order to save a few worthless relics from being swept away. Any system of thought or of education that cannot accommodate the intangibles, the things of the spirit that abide in the concepts of wholes, is doomed.

But worst of all is the absence of first principles. Whenever administrators or teachers come together the talk is largely about personal opinions and practices. Shockingly seldom is any reference ever made to a basic principle in education. Our own private and limited resources appear to be sufficient to meet the challenge of every conceivable exigency. Teachers who take themselves so seriously and admisistrators who base their exclusiveness on such shallow foundations are building for disaster.

What is meant by a basic principle? Before answering this question let us ask another upon the answer to which many things are contingent. Why is the pupil in school? The pupil may suspect he is there to get out from under foot at home, to perform a number of exercises outlined in textbooks, to help a teacher get through a lesson, or to get a handful of facts and information that can easily be forgotten later on. Remember that Whitehead, the philosopher, said that a merely well-informed man is the most useless bore on God's earth. The pupil may feel that he is being processed for good citizenship so that he will conform to the social pattern. He may think that he is there to prepare for a job – a job that may not exist when he is ready for it. He may wonder occasionally if he is there to endure the curse of unreality. One or all of these considerations, and others like them, may have some validity in the pupil's reflections, but the pupil is really in school to develop his mental faculties, not his physical prowess, vocal powers, or technical skill, but his mental faculties, his ability to think, feel, imagine, and wonder. He is there to think through the things of this world and to find out how they are linked together. He is there to stake a personal claim in the field of maturer judgments and better tastes. He is there to become a clear-headed and responsible person. "Language is one of the main activities of mind, and mind is the main part of personality." (Dr. Currey, *On Teaching English as a Foreign Language.*) The pupil's progress to his goal will be slow and insignificant unless his language and mental abilities move forward together. Now let us turn again to the original question.

What is meant by a basic principle? Here is an example

from the field of English. A masterpiece of imaginative literature is a work of art. It cannot be paraphrased, abridged, or simplified and retain its original character and artistic unity. Its form and content are inseparable. Recognition of this fact and adherence to it as a frame of reference in teaching would eliminate some texts from courses of study in both the elementary and the secondary school. Its influence on the teacher's method and his attitude to both the subject and the pupil would be profound. The teacher would soon discover that the completely subject-centred school is as absurd and inadequate as the completely child-centred school, and that his task is to bring the mind of the pupil near enough to the mind of the creative artist that the pupil may apprehend an experience akin to that of the artist's.

Another basic principle is this: subjects have different educational values and the values are not equal. If, for instance, language and numbers are not taught soundly and well, other subjects matter little because it is by means of one or the other of these subjects that other things are made intelligible. To this may be added the fact that a failure in mathematics is sometimes the result of a failure in language. Good education does not grow out of superficial contact with many subjects; it does grow out of sound understanding of a few. The pupil's progress should be determined not by the breadth of his selection among many subjects but rather by the depth to which his selecting mind can penetrate any one of them and win mastery over it. The mind selects what it can best digest, but just because a pupil appears uninterested is no sure sign that he lacks ability. Perhaps too often we underestimate his powers.

Recently a little girl named Janet came to Canada from Scotland and was entered in kindergarten in Toronto. The class was given the task of threading discs and straw alternately on a thread. Janet looked on, but refused to act.

After repeated urgings, explanations, and illustrations, the teacher finally asked her why she did not wish to do what all the other little girls were doing, and she received this terse and astonishing reply, "Since I turned three I've been knittin' my ain socks."

Although a literary masterpiece remains permanently fixed in form and content, language is constantly changing. New words like *smog*, *smaze*, and *smoil*, and new forms like *He upped the price* are coming in and old worn out words and forms that have survived their usefulness are disappearing. If the teacher accepts the premise that the native tongue is a living language and is constantly on the move, many of his theories concerning the teaching of grammar and composition, as they are practised today, will have to be changed. There is nothing wrong with formal grammar except that it is too formal and too unreal. It is too far removed from the living situations in which language is used. In English, today as always, thought relationship takes priority over linguistic relationship. Grammar is only a collection of descriptions of current usages, and we lack a good grammar of contemporary usage. There is nothing wrong with formal grammar except that it is outdated. Many of the rules set forth in some textbooks are wrong. "A pronoun," says one "is a word that takes the place of a noun." But surely a pronoun is a word that refers to the thing that a noun stands for. And why bother pestering a pupil below grade xi with such terms as correlative conjunction and conjunctive particle before he has mastery of the parts of speech and their function. There is nothing wrong with formal grammar, provided, of course, that we stop to think out the rules before speaking and writing, but we speak and write spontaneously, training our ear and eye, a long and arduous process, to keep our thoughts flowing in acceptable usage. This is the inner check. We learn early in life to be very sensitive regarding our decisions and our tastes. When we are ambiguous or stupid or fuzzy-minded we blush, but when we commit an error in grammar we laugh. And let it not be forgotten that many of the so-called faults or errors in the writing of pupils are never touched on by a grammar text. They are errors in logic, lapses in taste, changes in construction, ellipsis, ambiguities, or absurdities, etc.

The teaching of grammar is sterile unless what is learned is applied in a personal or living situation and is understood as a means of explaining things exactly and describing them accurately. It is sterile unless it helps the pupil to think more deeply about language and the way language can be used to express ideas. The methods by which it is taught are wrong unless they are conducive to the practice of better speaking and writing. Isolated lessons in grammar, so popular and so plentifully supplied, are educationally and pedagogically unsound. They deaden mental activity, they often prevent the pupil from thinking about language, and they take up much valuable time that could better be spent on the pupil's writing of straight-forward, continuous prose. In performing these isolated exercises in grammatical forms, word study, sentence structure, and paragraph construction, pupils sometimes become as clever as monkeys, and teachers find a sense of security and achievement. But are the pupils being trained to express their own thoughts and ideas better? Pedantry is not only an example of bad taste, but it is also irrelevant. And yet we teach grammar year after year throughout the middle grades, and wonder why it does not "stick."

Let us begin again with better methods. We can learn much from the teachers of painting and music. Give the pupils more practice in speaking and writing, and give more instruction informally and incidentally. More real grammar can be taught effectively by this method than was ever derived from the old method. When points in grammar come up, let the pupils think out their own rules, and in their note books write their own findings about usage as they go along. What is needed is a more intelligent and intelligible use of grammar. Encourage the pupils to write more frequently and at greater length so that they can develop a feeling for language.

A feeling for language will never be developed by taking up the meanings of hundreds of big words. What is more useful to know is how to use a few words more exactly and imaginatively. It is better to be able to use correctly such simple words as *good*, *great*, and *grand* than to carry around a word like *grandiose*, only to misuse it. Frequent application of such methods as have been suggested will bring language alive, and liberate the pupil from the confinement of blithering idiocy. He may become a person.

But what hope is there of success if the teacher is not free to develop his personality, his mental powers, and his professional prestige to the full? It is the classroom teacher who is chiefly responsible for the pupil's formal education. He is present when the two-way radiation takes place. Left alone to work out his own salvation and given full responsibility, he will soon outgrow the false belief that whatever succeeds must be good and wise and true, and begin to look for basic principles. To succeed, however, he must be confronted by classes considerably reduced in numbers.

2. *Beyond Excellence*

A philosophy of education worth the name cannot be founded on the statistics of research or the ideas lectured about in graduate schools, but it may be developed by the teacher in the classroom where tested ideas may be institutionalized. The danger exists, however, in too much professionalism. The professionals are paid off in the prestige of their profession. When I go to a medical doctor, to a lawyer or to an engineer for advice, I hope I am meeting a mature human being first and an expert technician second. When I meet a teacher I am first concerned with his qualities as a human being, and secondly with the qualities of his teaching. At all levels teachers run the risk of being dismissed as damned snobs. By harping stupidly on professionalism they may win a self-imposed dignity and detachment and lose touch with the world of reality. The higher we raise our standards, the better will be the candidates we attract. The teacher image today is completely different from what it was twenty years ago. A contemporary caricaturist would be hard put to it to catch that image on the wing. Not professionalism, but leadership should be the aim.

Today the fully qualified, experienced, and approved secondary school teacher is an expert in the knowledge and skill required to teach his subject well. He is an idealist who believes that there is power latent in his proper teaching of his subject that may save the world from catastrophe. He is also a realist who knows that not everyone can benefit from his teaching. He knows that learning for many requires great mental effort and a sound motivating reason, and yet undaunted he struggles cheerfully onward with the blind hope of an Arnold as described in *Rugby Chapel*. Patient, tolerant, reliable, loyal, conscientious, he lives out his philosophy of life from day to day in and around the school. He is an expert, and he tries to be efficient. Given half a chance to claim the modest indulgence and cooperation of his pupils, he can get them through the grades and through the examinations and dispatch them into the world with a required amount of information and mental and manual skills.

The curriculum is intended to deepen insights and sharpen intellects, to provide background for many trades and professions, and to acquaint youth with the customs of the tribe. The universities carry all these potentials to a higher level and leave them there. But it is staff that makes a university, not buildings, nor libraries, nor graduate schools, nor research departments. It is staff and staff alone that makes a university. The secondary school is consequently confronted by responsibilities it has not entertained before. Both the teacher and the principal have new problems and new responsibilities.

Of all men's attributes it appears that his intellect has, in the process of his education, always been singled out for attention. Education and nimbleness of intellect are perhaps for some people synonymous terms. A premium has been placed on knowledge rather than on wisdom and judgment. Should nourishing the mind of man or triggering his intellect be the proper end of education?

In 1920 H. G. Wells proclaimed "Human history becomes more and more a race between education and catastrophe." Looking at the gadgety world of today one may wonder if education and catastrophe are in competition or co-operation. So long as man's cleverness is aimed at the moon, we have only the loss of our natural resources to lament. When it is aimed at this planet our human resources are in jeopardy. As teachers at all levels we have a responsibility that our predecessors never had to contemplate or face. The search for truth may end in one blinding moment of truth.

Through the ages, the training and the development of the human intellect has been a paramount concern. Knowledge of physical law or of moral law or of both, and facts and ideas accepted or acquired, have provided food for the exercise of thought and the means of education. Reason, faith, will, taste, insight, and conscience have all in varying degrees played a modifying role in shaping the educational ends of the various ages. The early Egyptians hoped to produce by means of education the good nobleman; the early Greek, the good Greek citizen; Plato, the good state; Aristotle, the self-governing citizen; the early Christian, the good Christian; Thomas Aquinas, the rational Christian; Erasmus, the free citizen; Martin Luther, the informed Christian; Francis Bacon, the scientific man; John Milton, the emancipated citizen; John Locke, the cultured gentleman; Immanuel Kant, the balanced mind; Jean Jacques Rousseau, the incorruptible man; Pestalozzi, Froebel, and Herbart, the socially adjusted citizen; and John Dewey, the adaptable citizen. In our own time, Sir Richard Livingstone has recommended excellence as a goal to be sought in and through education: and it may be assumed that he means excellence in everything that we are presently doing, including intelligence testing.

After 10,000 years of civilization and nearly 2,000 years of Christianity, man has learned very little concerning how to live with himself and with his neighbour; and right here is the crux of the whole matter. On man the individual depends the welfare of each one of us, socially, economically, and politically. Education for all capable of participating in it, each to his highest level, is the greatest need of our democratic time.

No one will deny that there is a fair amount of violence, vandalism, and vagrancy abroad in society. Some teachers will say that police forces are maintained to deal with these diseases. Within the school, disciplining codes are established and cannot be broken with impunity. The operation of the machine is assured. The ritual of education at all levels is preserved. Parents and pupils accept this as the best of all possible routines. Children go in at one end and young men and women come out at the other. They obey the rules, pass examinations with varying degrees of success, occasionally participate in genuine intellectual and emotional experiences, make important decisions, and subscribe to a modicum of proper judgments. There is nothing seriously wrong with this procedure, except that pupils and students live a good deal of their real lives outside of it. They conform to the rules of the game and go their way, often untouched because unchallenged, ignoring the lessons learned at school and university because they are ignorant of how these lessons relate to life.

Consider the innumerable journeys made by pupils in the name of education into the intuitive and imaginative world created by Shakespeare, and wonder why these insights are lost sight of in the study of the world around us. Consider the innumerable objective analyses made in the school of historical, mathematical, and scientific facts, and recall how quickly they are set aside as of no account in the arena of daily affairs when in the street of life we are confronted by a political opinion, a religious conviction, or a profile and complexion that differs from our own. If mathematics should illustrate any fact, it should make clear the folly of trying to get something for nothing. If science can teach us anything, it should make clear that we are not in ultimate control of our own fate. At a football game or in a political campaign one may wonder if the educational system serves any useful purpose at all.

I am not suggesting a revolutionary change, but I wish to point out that now we must put forth a new effort to humanize education, if we are to use the educational system not only for the quickening of the intellect, but also for the development of responsible persons.

If the educational system from bottom to top is largely concerned with the dispensing of fragments of unrelated knowledge and the practising of a variety of unrelated skills, it is falling far short of its potential and its purpose. The tools of education brought to bear on each one of us in our daily lives will render important decisions inescapable. In man's experiencing of fear and hope, despair and aspirations, through the ages, as communicated to him through words and numbers and set before him in the materials of the curriculum, lie points of view and problems, solved and unsolved. Properly presented and examined, the curriculum can be quickly changed from a rat race to a race to be run for genuine prizes that everyone may make his own.

Before a man is allowed to work underground in a mine, he must take a brief course of training in personal responsibility. Uppermost in that training is his responsibility for the mate who works with him. Here is an example of sound, realistic, and practical education. The same man above ground may, however, be a menace to his fellow motorist on the highway.

Again, some advertising used on radio and television today is very clever in both content and execution, but entirely irresponsible. The same is true of some programmes other than those called commercials. No thought is given to the possible evil effects of such deceptions and deluded thuggery. What must be the subconscious response of some people to doctors and lawyers who never lose a case? How much of present day apathy in the world may be traced to the will to death that has saturated the literature of two decades? Is there no spring time, but only autumn for the spirit of man to endure?

If responsibility can be inculcated in one area, it can be developed in others. In education many of the tools are ready to hand. But first let us take another squint at the intellect.

> And men should know that from nothing else but from the brain come joys, delights, laughter and jests, and sorrows, griefs, despondency and lamentations. And by this in an especial manner, we acquire wisdom and knowledge, and see and hear and know what are foul and what are fair, what sweet and what unsavory .... And by the same organ we become mad and delirious and fears and terrors assail us, some by night and some by day, and dreams and untimely wanderings, and cares that are not suitable and ignorance of present circumstances, desuetude and unskillfulness. All these things we endure from the brain, when it is not healthy, but is more hot, more cold, more moist, or more dry than

natural, or when it suffers any other preternatural and unusual affliction.

That was written by Hippocrates, a physician, about 400 B.C. What he was saying was bluntly this: "that man should know that from nothing else but from the brain come" all man's behaviour patterns, not from his heart or his glands, or his spleen, but from his brain. About the same time an Aristotelian notion that reason and feeling resided in the heart became popular, and this error has been here to plague man ever since. Mechanistically, man has been partitioned into many parts – truly a man of parts – with blame for misdemeanours allotted accordingly. But if the brain is the seat of man's judgment, reason, will, tastes, and faith – his conscience in short – it is improper to hold his glands or that intricate muscle, the heart, which has no power to reason or make judgments, responsible for his conduct. When a person flies into a passion, as they say, it is his mind that is in passion, not the heart. He is out of balance, off centre, eccentric, irresponsible – and a strange coincidence may show him to be a student of psychology.

In the brain resides the unity of personality, and the cultivation of the whole personality is the work of education at all levels. Man is free to think as he pleases, but he must bear responsibility for his thoughts. Whether we like it or not, we are not only teachers of the two great languages of words and numbers, but the nourishers as well of the maturing mind. What are some of the signs of that maturing?

The time and the nature of maturation differ with every individual and with every stage in his development. There are, nevertheless, some signs of maturing that are common to most youngsters in the various stages of their development. Boys and girls are often deeply moved by acts of courage, sacrifice, fortitude, or love, and such experiences are not reserved for those alone who are thought to be exceptionally bright or clever. And who has not been amazed at some of the searching questions that young people ask? Maturity is reflected in the character of one's interests, curiosity, and enjoyment. It is forecast in one's tastes, decisions, and judgments. If a boy shows a little too much independence of spirit he may be considered impudent or aloof when all that he is trying to do is to break free from apron strings, escape from the forcible feeding of opinions, withdraw from the impact of mis-understood judgments, or refuse to be typed, classified or standardized, and rendered functional. Such behaviour is nothing less than a sign of his maturing, a manifestation of his desire to think things through for himself, to assert his right to individuality. Unless he is ready to take risks and make mistakes, experiences will profit him little.

The ability to distinguish between what is important and what is irrelevant in a collection of related details in any subject is one sign of maturity. A readiness to cope with difficulties, to attack a problem and try by his own efforts and without goading to solve it, is another. Mature young people usually find in their school work something that they like to do, something for which they are pleased to make sacrifices. The others must be helped to find the problems. A subtle and pervasive sense of humour is another mark of maturity, and its expression a proof of confident articulation. When immediate needs begin to give place to ultimate ends, a sense of responsibility is developing.

The search for maturity is a search for individuality, a search that is self-starting, self-directed, self-confident, self-critical, self-controlled, and self-poised. Youth's deep-est desire is to grow up, to find a spinal theme for the personal life, a core of meaning in the midst of a continent of rapidly changing experiences. It is a striving after whole-ness. Every sane person feels a need to belong, to play a part in the scheme of things, but he also feels a need for independence of thought and action. If he is to stand up to the crowded controversies of daily life and carry out his duties and responsibilities as he sees them, he must have the support of quietness and strength at the centre of his own personality.

By the very nature of things each one of us is born to live on a horizontal plane of time and space. And yet within each one is the urge to escape from these limiting boundaries, to find identity on a vertical pattern, to transcend the physical world and find a satisfying mental life beyond it without losing touch with it. Mind is the chief component of personality, and the creative activity of the mind operates in a vertical pattern with only superficial connection with either time or place. All great achievements in both the arts and the sciences are evidence of this fact. Thus everyone is free to make of his life an artistic masterpiece. Everyone is responsible for the pattern he makes of living.

The chief business of the teacher is to prepare the conditions for the pupil's growth. He is the catalyst who induces thought and stirs up the mind to look at things differently, originally. The teacher encourages the mind to grow by what it feeds on.

To develop mature habits of mind requires a framework within which the making of decisions can prevail and the powers of taste and judgment be exercised. The core subjects of the curriculum provide that framework. When history, for example, is studied for the problems it presents rather than for the period it comprises, it becomes alive. Problems are seen as wholes in vertical patterns with beginning, middle, and end. History then ceases to be chiefly a series of events in horizontal progression, unrelated to some central meaning or purpose. Likewise every masterpiece of literature or mathematical solution or scientific experiment is a unity – a unit of experience constructed out of and upon some intuitive and imaginative premise, a unit that remains open at both ends. Artists and scientists are both working and writing for the record, not just to amuse themselves. They are all making important statements about their experiences. They are anxious to help us see more clearly and to understand better what we see.

The plays of Shakespeare and the novels of Hardy are not just stories that run on and on from one event to another — and then, and then, and then — but problems in the study of man in his earthly predicament. Such problems, as set forth in either of the two languages of communication, words and numbers, are perennially new and important.

To transfer mere living into an art requires a pattern — not a fixed plan, but a flexible pattern of thinking. Every person has problems of all kinds, and most of these problems stem from the fact that they do not know where they are going or where they wish to go. But make a pattern of life, constructed vertically on a moveable premise and the problems begin to sort themselves out and to dissolve in solutions of discrimination, orderliness, confidence, enthusiasm and a will to live. This has nothing to do with guidance as presently practised. It has everything to do with the study of the arts and the sciences as patterns of mental achievement on which problems of all kinds have been either resolved or still await solutions. This is patterned living.

As teachers it is our job to dig out these problems, to mine the hard rock until it gives up the good ore, to test its quality for reality, to refine it for relatedness, and to offer it in the market of personal responsiblity. There is plenty of room for improvement in the present curriculum, but any good teacher can dig out of almost any material a useful lesson.

In certain parts of the world today the educational race is fast and furious and mechanistic. Schools and universities are hothouses for the cultivation of hybrid intellectuals, plastic people useful to the machine. We are not competitors in that race. We are not so sure that we are always right. We are not so sure that our personal resources are alone sufficient to solve all the problems confronting us. We need one another and we are responsible for one another.

The mountain peaks of excellence are stark and sterile, and capped by clouds of selfishness and snobbery. If we follow the sunlit valleys of reality, relatedness, and responsibility, we may pass beyond the peaks of excellence to behold new horizons of experience where the pattern of each individual life may have personal meaning and communal significance. Should we succeed, the educational system for the first time in history will have played a part in preserving peace and inculcating freedom.

Schooling might well contain a study of elementary economics, anthropology, the life sciences, and even philosophy. It would help students greatly in their work and in their contacts with others to know a little about why people think and act the way they do. In terms of reality, relatedness, and responsibility, such courses would represent a new adventure in education at the secondary level. Such innovations might in time affect the whole system for the better. Collectively they form a plan which, like the pattern of a masterpiece, is open at both ends.

The art of responsible living is first among the arts that everyone can practise today, and this art can be learned as easily as any other art in the classrooms of Ontario. An entirely new, fresh, and enlightening view of life and learning is available to everyone who can learn to behold life and learning with the synoptic vision of an artist. Then the language and the literature of all the subjects we teach, whether we be confronted by a Latin sentence or a lathe, take on new significance and meaning. Problems fall into focus. Brains begin to count. Then the mental life appears to be the only real, reliable, and rewarding one to cultivate in ourselves and in others as we interpret the experiences of the creative thinkers of the past, and in the light of them try to organize the patterns of our own. As Jacques Maritain, the French philosopher, has declared, "Great poets and thinkers are the foster-fathers of intelligence. Cut off from them, we are simply barbarous."

3. *Some Recommendations*

How can the present dilemma in Canadian education be resolved? How can common sense in education be restored?

It is time to place an embargo on the importation of American education theories. Our neighbours to the south are in no way to blame. Their problems and purposes are quite different from our own. Their criticisms of their own conditions are not directed at Canada, but our local opportunists, anxious to attract attention to themselves, cultivate an appetite for foreign theories to enhance their prestige with the politicians.

In 1943, for instance, a small but influential group of "educators" in Ontario suddenly became enamoured of progressivism and a variety of other "isms" rampant at that time in the u.s.a., and introduced "guidance" as a formal part of the curriculum. Since then a steady eroding of education by sociology — the science that treats of the structure of society — has followed. Consultants, psychologists, sociologists, and so-called research people are now attempting to crowd the teachers of subject matter, such as language, mathematics, science, history, and geography, into the background as fashions outmoded. Evidently it has become more important that a student "adjust" to society than that he learn how to read, write, and calculate. Apparently radio and television will, meanwhile, keep him informed of his rights and his reasons for his behaviour.

Recently a disc jockey who had dropped out of school at Grade 10 strove to add to his popularity by denouncing the school as a jail and the teachers as jailers. His protest gave ample proof of his immaturity and brazen conceit.

But why this sudden shift of emphasis from education to sociology? Thirty years ago boys and girls solved their problems, personal and educational, in their own particular way without external meddling. Some studied, and passed their examinations; others, who were side-tracked into other pursuits, went another way, some to succeed and some to drift. People are different. Not all are capable of enduring the rigours of intellectual pursuits. But surely boys and girls today are not so different from those of past generations! Whence comes this unusual surge to protest? Why does a pupil seek a guider's assistance to adjust to society, to the standard classroom, or to the authority of a principal or a teacher of an academic subject? Does he drop out in order to quench a thirst for rebellion, to rid himself of some imaginary guilt complex, or to foster a feeling of alienation? Does he feel harassed as a slave of a system that denies him personal identity?

Boys and girls are just as responsible and resourceful as ever they were. Why, then, should some people claim that book learning is obsolete, that the school is irrelevant to the needs of contemporary society, and that the only valid school is the "open" school in which pupils choose what they will study, when they will study, how they will study, where they will study, and from whom they will learn? Such freedom is a fantasy without foundation in reality. Then why import obsolete theories discarded by foreign educators on either side of the Atlantic? Why turn the school into a clinic for the study or certification of the human species? Or is this the route to socialism, a way to instant Utopia designed by pretentious radicals for their own advancement?

The aim of education in a democracy is not, as in Russia

and China at present, the preservation of a static social structure. A social system forced on a people from above stifles initiative. Throughout history, improvement in the human condition has been initiated by individuals possessed of ability to think, reflect, invent, discover, and create. An important purpose of the school is to affirm, profess, and project the knowledge and experience of that human heritage, and not merely to provide a forum for social ills. The time is long overdue to re-establish the priority and prestige of education over sociology.

The school, furthermore, is not a "fun" place; neither is learning a "fun" thing! The solving of a problem in mathematics is not the same as learning how to skate or swim. The study of a Shakespearean drama bears little resemblance to the viewing of a movie version of the same material. The study of the delightfully humane essays of Peter McArthur bears little resemblance to a perusal of any current digest of articles. The content, the challenges, and the rewards are all different. Today we are urged to approve of the educational values of television, but those values are largely sociological rather than educational. Humanity, however, will never be redeemed by sociology, but it may be nourished by education.

In the preparation of teachers there is a movement on foot today to eliminate the study of the materials and methods of teaching and to replace it by lectures about teaching, and all this in spite of the fact that the lecture is the poorest method devised for the participation of students and the learning of anything. Its emphasis is on the dissemination of opinions or the presentation of statistical proof of the obvious rather than on the experiencing of a "head or hand" skill. Yet only the other day a prominent educational administrator proclaimed that a good teacher could teach a hundred pupils at one and the same time. Heaven help the thousands of good teachers who have for years been asking in vain for smaller classes.

Finally it is time to divert the millions of dollars assigned for irrelevant research with sociological methods to the preparation of more and better teachers. It is time to reassert some Canadian nationalism in the educational system and reunite learning with life.

Appendix

In the light of the foregoing, some students, teachers, and parents may be provoked to consider and discuss their responses to the following questions. The answers to many of these questions may be found in the preceding pages.

A. 1. Why is the student in school?

2. How can a student's imagination and sense of wonder be awakened and developed?

3. What are the chief signs that a student is maturing mentally?

4. What are the ingredients of mental pollution, and what are their sources?

5. What are some of the horrendous effects of inflated egos?

6. What are the educational hazards of exposure to an opinionated mind?

7. In the event of a national catastrophe how much of the educational system becomes essential, and how much expendable?

8. How is myth related to reality?

9. What special educational values and advantages has the "question and answer" method, as opposed to the Socratic and other methods of teaching?

10. When and how may a senior pupil share with a

teacher in the intruction of a class? What are the advantages and dangers latent in such a practice?

11. What are the main points of resemblance and of difference between (a) sociology and education, (b) art and propaganda and (c) literary masterpieces and "whodunits"?

12. For decades some educators have advocated a need for "socializing" the student. With what results?

13. How can respect for others be inculcated in a person who has no self-respect?

14. When does vulgarity become a form of violence?

15. How can good taste be cultivated, and when does it become tyrannical?

16. Which is more significant, the biological or the psychological composition of the human brain?

B. 1. What singular values accrue from the study of English literature?

2. What are the differences between literary experience and literary appreciation?

3. How can a case be argued for "taking up a poem" rather than "teaching a poem"?

4. When studying a poem, what part may be played by the following: the biography of the poet; a comparison of the poem with others in the same form or with the poet's discarded attempts; and the teacher's or the student's personal experience?

5. What defence can be made for (a) examining differences between poetry and prose as they deal with similar material, and (b) studying the "influences" of earlier poets on the poet under discussion?

6. How can interest in poetry be aroused in a class predisposed to dislike the subject?

7. How can a knowledge of metrical structure be used to enhance the meaning of a poem?

8. In how many ways can poetry be distinguished from prose, and poetry from verse?

9. When and how can literary forms best be introduced?

10. In how many ways does a short story differ from an essay?

11. What values should accrue to a student from the study of a novel that is regarded as a classic?

12. What are the relative values of reading a novel such as *David Copperfield, Wuthering Heights* or *Far from the Madding Crowd* and viewing a movie version of the same subject?

13. Should literature be studied as a collection of ideas, or as an art, or both?

14. How can the "intensive" and the "extensive" study of literature be distinguished from each other?

15. In studying a literary masterpiece should emphasis be given to one component, such as rhyme, rhythm, form, idea, or image, at a time, or to all components as they occur?

16. What are the differences between "vertical pattern" and "horizontal plane"?

17. Why are the great writers our most practical and least harmful psychologists?

18. How can the study of literature contribute to a reader's philosophy of life?

19. What are the advantages and disadvantages of memorizing "purple" passages?

20. When and how can (a) supplementary reading be encouraged; (b) "sight work" be used; (c) contemporary

periodicals be introduced; (d) a school magazine be published?

21. What benefits should students of each grade (9 to 13) receive from their study of English literature?

22. What subject matter should comprise a minimum essential for the study of English literature at the secondary school level?

C. 1. What unique values has "dramatics" in education?

2. How can "theatre" and "dramatics" be integrated with the study of literature?

3. Why is informal classroom "acting," even if crude, worth-while?

4. In the study of a Shakespearean play, how can the sense of drama (The play's the thing) be maintained?

5. What are the relative values of analysing the structure of the plot and the making of character sketches when studying a Shakespearean play?

6. What are the differences between "dramatic experience" and "poetic experience"?

D. 1. What are the essentials of "language study" that may effect improvement in a student's command of his mother tongue?

2. What arguments can be advanced for the teaching of English grammar, and how can it best be taught?

3. How can acceptable standards of usage in speech and writing be secured?

4. How can the student's vocabulary be increased and improved?

5. What types of language practice best enable students to make use of the formal rules of grammar?

6. Why should students be urged to accept personal responsibility for their own speech and writing?

7. Of what use is it to encourage students to write well when many of them are unlikely to do much writing after they have left school?

8. What are some of the many common fallacies apparent in the teaching of creative writing?

9. How can intelligent and effective public speaking best be practised?

10. How can the standards of speaking in class be improved?

11. Why should students be encouraged to write verse?

12. Should the study of literature and the practice of literary composition lead to the clarification of personal identity, or social adaptability, or both?

E. Parents, teachers, and students who are seriously interested in fostering the study of good literature will find the following books useful and interesting:

P. Gurrey: *The Appreciation of Poetry*

Leavis and Thompson: *Culture and Environment*

C. C. Lewis: *The Abolition of Man*

Dorothy L. Sayers: *The Mind of the Maker*

M. C. Bradbrook: *Elizabethan Stage Conditions*

B. L. Joseph: *Elizabethan Acting*

William Empson: *Seven Types of Ambiguity*

E. M. W. Tillyard: *Poetry, Direct and Oblique*

B. C. Diltz: *The Sense of Wonder*

W. M. Urban: *Language and Reality*

Acknowledgements

"The Pool" by George Johnston, from *The Cruising Auk*, Oxford University Press, 1959. Reprinted by permission of the publisher.

"Ellesmereland" by Earle Birney. Reprinted by permission of the author and McClelland and Stewart Limited.

"To Emily Dickinson" by John Moffitt. Reprinted by permission of the author from *This Narrow World*, Dodd, Mead and Company, © 1956, 1957, 1958 by John Moffitt.

"The Road Not Taken," "The Tuft of Flowers," and "Questioning Faces" by Robert Frost. Reprinted from *The Poetry of Robert Frost*, Edward Connery Lathem (ed.), Holt, Rinehart and Winston, Inc. by permission of the publisher.

"The Scarecrow" by Walter de la Mare. Reprinted by permission of The Literary Trustees of Walter de la Mare and the Society of Authors as their representative.

"Mine-sweepers" by Rudyard Kipling, from *The Mayor of Casterbridge* by Thomas Hardy, "The Shark" by E. J. Pratt, and "Before the World Was Made" by William Butler Yeats. Reprinted by permission of the Macmillan Company of Canada Limited.